Julie Stafford's
Wok Cookbook

PENGUIN BOOKS

Acknowledgement
The author and publisher would like to thank Market Import, 19 Morey Street,
Armadale, Victoria 3143, Australia, for the use of plates and napkins in the
photographs in this book.

PENGUIN BOOKS

Published by the Penguin Group
Penguin Books Ltd, 27 Wrights Lane, London W8 5TZ, England
Penguin Books USA Inc., 375 Hudson Street, New York, New York 10014, USA
Penguin Books Australia Ltd, Ringwood, Victoria, Australia
Penguin Books Canada Ltd, 10 Alcorn Avenue, Toronto, Ontario, Canada M4V 3B2
Penguin Books (NZ) Ltd. 182–190 Wairau Road, Auckland 10, New Zealand

Penguin Books Ltd, Registered Offices: Harmondsworth, Middlesex, England

First published in Australia by Viking 1996
Published in Penguin Books 1997
10 9 8 7 6 5 4 3 2 1

Typeset in 9/14pt Rotis Semi Serif by Post Typesetters, Queensland, Australia
Illustrated by Michelle Macdonald
Photography by Mark Chew
Printed in Australia by Australian Print Group, Maryborough, Victoria, Australia

Front cover photograph
Chow mein of vegetables (page 76).

Contents

Preface

In 1976 I travelled to China and spent the most incredible six weeks in city and rural areas sampling the gastronomic delights of each province. It was my first experience of Chinese food cooked traditionally in the wok. Many of the dishes consisted of braised, steamed or deep-fried vegetables simply combined with small amounts of meat, chicken, duck or fish, and usually accompanied by aromatic rice or noodles. The intriguing thing about the cuisine was the slightly undercooked nature of the vegetables, and the delicate or intense flavours that identified each dish with its region.

I returned home to Australia with a new interest in food and flavours, finding that the traditional 'three veg and meat' meal, the grill and the roast dinners of my childhood had lost much of their appeal. Wok cooking quickly became a favourite of mine and it remains so today. With the development of a more health-conscious attitude towards eating, wok cooking has become one of the easiest, fastest and healthiest ways of combining compatible ingredients to achieve sensational flavours and memorable eating experiences. It fits perfectly with the Taste of Life philosophy of a low-fat, high-fibre, low-sugar, low-salt diet, and today's trend towards lighter fast foods that not only look and taste good but are good for us.

This is a style of cooking that cuts back the fat and integrates the flavours of fresh ingredients, especially vegetables. Extra flavour comes from the addition of herbs, spices, wine, stock, and small quantities of the widely available commercial sauces and condiments. Within minutes of tossing the ingredients together, novice cooks can become the star of their very own kitchen.

This book is intended only as a beginner's guide. I have purposely chosen ingredients that are widely available but if you have access to the more unusual ingredients found at Asian markets or in specialty stores you can substitute these for some of the Australian or European ingredients I have suggested. If you do not own a wok, I recommend that you save up for one. A traditional stainless-steel wok is not expensive, and even the best electric woks are not really expensive today. You will certainly get better results from a wok than a large flat-bottomed frying pan.

Many of the recipes in this book were created while I was holidaying at Point Lonsdale in Victoria, where our family gathers for the annual summer break. Fast, healthy meals, using the wonderfully varied local produce – especially fresh fish from Queenscliff – were produced in a matter of minutes for the ravenous surfers (who once upon a time were content to sit on the front beach and build sand castles!). The simplicity of these recipes and the fun of combining all the ingredients in the one cooking utensil reinforced for me the true value of my own wonderful electric wok.

I hope you will enjoy these recipes as much as my family, my friends and I have, and that you will take the time to explore this style of cooking further. Happy wokking!

Recipe books are so much fun to work on, but the best part of all is taste-testing the recipes. I want to say a big thankyou to my official Wok Taste Test Team, who not only sampled the dishes and offered some great new ideas, but also suggested some catchy titles for the book.

Bruce: Wok My Way
Cassie: Take a Wok on the Wild Side
Timothy: Wok's Up Doc?
Ann: Stand by Your Wok
Denis: Wok like a Man
Sarah: Wok a Beauty
Jessica: Wok Around the Clock
Rebecca: Wok to the Future
Pa: Wok On!

Special thanks go to my wonderful typist, Vicki O'Keeffe, to Julie Gibbs at Viking, and to my editor, Margaret Barrett, who continue to give me so much support in publishing my contributions to healthier eating.

Introduction

The traditional wok is a simple round-bottomed or flat-bottomed concave, deep-sided cooking utensil mainly used to stirfry evenly sized morsels of food in a little oil, stock or water. Cooking in a well-seasoned steel wok or one with a non-stick surface enables you to dry-stirfry the ingredients without the need for oil, stock or water in the initial stages. Ingredients are simply put into a hot wok and cooked quickly over high heat with flavour-enhancing spices and herbs. Stocks, condiments and a thickening agent are added at the very last minute.

The wok cooking technique is to continuously toss all the food within the wok so that it comes into contact with the hot surface of the utensil but does not stay long enough to stick or burn. It takes just minutes for delicate flavours to develop. For more concentrated flavours, the wok is covered with a lid and the food is allowed to simmer gently.

The high temperature required for wok cooking seals in the natural flavours of vegetables and marinated meats. Vegetables remain crunchy in texture, are vibrant in colour, and retain a great deal of their nutritional goodness. You can simmer a favourite soup recipe in a covered wok, or create a curry dish in a variety of delicious creamy sauces. With the addition of a steaming rack, the wok can even be used to steam a whole fish.

The right wok for you

There is a wide range of woks to choose from. You'll find them in Asian food shops and markets, and at department stores. Woks come in all sizes and are made of various materials. My advice to you is to choose the one that best suits your main cooking appliance – gas or electric – and your cooking style.

If you have electric hotplates you will need a heavy-duty steel, flat-bottomed, deep-sided wok to conduct heat effectively. Remember to cook on the highest temperature setting and remove the wok from the hotplate as soon as the food is cooked. With a gas stove you can be a little more flexible. The wok can be heavy-duty or lightweight steel with a flat or rounded bottom. It is best to have a deep-sided wok so that the flames can move around the base and up the sides to distribute heat evenly.

Woks that have a non-stick surface are particularly suitable for low-fat cooking. You can stirfry the food on the seasoned non-stick surface without actually cooking in oil, or simmer the food in a little water, wine or flavoursome stock. I have used the Breville electric non-stick wok to cook the recipes featured in this book. It is a very easy wok to cook in and requires little cleaning. The model I use has a 2000-watt heating element that doubles back on itself and heats up faster than woks with only a single-ring element. It also distributes heat more evenly and retains it longer, and is thermostatically controlled for multiple heat selections. Most electric woks are elegantly designed and have tight-fitting lids that lock in the flavour and goodness of the food. These woks can be carried directly to the table for serving.

Seasoning your wok

Steel woks
'Seasoning' a wok with oil gives it a protective coating and adds to the flavour of your dishes. You must also season the wok thoroughly before using it for the first time. A brand-new steel wok has a protective coating on its cooking surfaces that needs to be removed before you can use it. Heat the wok and wipe canola oil over the inner surface with a paper towel. Continue doing this until the surface begins to shine and the paper comes away clean. After using your wok, rinse it under hot water and remove any food residue with a sponge. Reheat the wok, add a little canola oil, and wipe the inside with a paper towel. Always season your steel wok before using it, as well as before putting it away. If there is any sign of rust, treat it to the same thorough seasoning that you gave your wok when it was new.

Non-stick woks
One of the advantages of using an electric non-stick wok is that seasoning it is a very easy, mess-free task. You'll need only the tiniest amount of canola oil on a tissue. Rub the inside of the wok with the lightly oiled tissue and wipe off any excess oil before cooking. This seals and protects the cooking surface, enabling you to dry stirfry the food without needing more oil. After cooking, simply rinse the wok under hot water, wipe over with a soft sponge and dry thoroughly. The non-stick surface does not need to be seasoned between uses.

To add extra flavour to your recipes you can rub a clove of garlic or a small piece of ginger over the cooking surface after seasoning your wok.

Ten steps to success

1 To create the best flavours and the most visibly pleasing results, always use the freshest of ingredients.

2 Cut all the main ingredients into small pieces of similar shape and size so that they cook fast and evenly.

3 Season your wok with no more than 1 teaspoon of canola oil. Use a tissue to distribute the oil evenly over the cooking surface of the wok, and wipe away any excess before cooking.

4 Before you start, have all your ingredients prepared and laid out on the bench in the right order. Wok cooking is very fast cooking. There is no time to look for that forgotten item or prepare ingredients as you go. An extra sixty seconds can mean the difference between a perfect dish and an overcooked one.

5 Make sure your wok is very hot before you add the first ingredients or the result will be a stew. Drain marinated foods very well before adding them to the wok: cold, wet food will also make the temperature drop quickly and stew the food rather than dry stirfry it.

6 Use a flat wooden spatula for stirring the ingredients in the wok. Lift the food against the hot sides of the wok, wait a few seconds for the heat to build up again, and repeat the process.

7 As you add each new ingredient to the wok you need to work fast, continuously turning over and tossing the contents. It is an excellent idea to have some extra stock or water nearby to add if the ingredients are cooking too fast or beginning to stick to the wok.

8 It is best to slightly undercook the ingredients rather than completely cook them. Because of the high temperature used, the food will continue to cook even after you remove the wok from its heat source.

9 The food is cooked when it changes colour. Meat and fish lose their raw exterior colour, onion, garlic and ginger become white, vegetables become vibrant in colour, and sauces change from opaque to a shiny glaze. To be perfectly sure, taste-test one or two ingredients. Adjust seasonings to your liking at this stage.

10 Have on hand an extra tablespoon of cornflour mixed with 2 tablespoons of water, in case the completed dish is too runny. Quickly stir through just a little at a time to reach the desired consistency.

Chicken and fish wok-style

The spices, sauces and cuisines of exotic cultures turn chicken and fish into quick and easy gourmet dishes in your wok. Here are some recipes to inspire you – the possibilities are endless.

Chicken chow mein

Serves 4

250 g thin spaghetti
400 g chicken fillet, skin and fat removed
1 tablespoon sweet chilli sauce
1 tablespoon dry sherry
1 tablespoon low-salt soy sauce
1 onion, peeled and sliced
125 g sugar peas, topped and tailed
125 g red capsicum, seeded and sliced
125 g asparagus spears, halved
125 g mushrooms, thinly sliced
1 cup Chicken Stock (page 118) or water
125 g bean sprouts
1 tablespoon cornflour
2 tablespoons water

Preparation

Season wok with canola oil.

Cut chicken into bite-size pieces and combine with chilli sauce, sherry and soy sauce and marinate for at least two hours. Drain juices and reserve.

Combine all vegetables except bean sprouts.

Combine cornflour and water and mix together well.

Cooking

Cook spaghetti until tender; drain and keep warm.

Stirfry chicken in a hot, dry wok for about two minutes or until it loses its raw exterior colour. Remove chicken from wok and keep warm.

Add vegetables, chicken stock and reserved juices; cover, and simmer for about a minute or until vegetables are just tender and a vibrant colour.

Add cornflour mixture, stir and cook until sauce thickens slightly.

Add chicken and cook until it is warmed through.

Add bean sprouts and lightly stirfry to combine.

Arrange spaghetti on a hot platter and top with the chicken chow mein. Serve with a tossed green salad.

Mandarin chicken
with macadamia nuts

Serves 4–6

½ cup chopped macadamia nuts
600 g chicken fillet, skin and fat removed
1 onion, peeled and cut into thin wedges
2 teaspoons Ginger Paste (page 117)
2 teaspoons grated mandarin rind
250 g bean sprouts
2 mandarins, peeled and segmented
sprigs of fresh coriander

Sauce

1 tablespoon mirin

1 cup fresh mandarin juice

1 tablespoon cornflour

Preparation

Season wok with canola oil.

Cut chicken into bite-size pieces and combine with onion, ginger paste and mandarin rind. Allow to stand for at least thirty minutes. Drain and reserve juices.

Combine sauce ingredients and mix together well.

Cooking

Put macadamia nuts into a dry, hot wok and stirfry until golden brown. Set aside.

Add chicken, onion, ginger paste and mandarin rind to a dry, hot wok and stirfry for about two minutes or until chicken loses its raw exterior colour and onion becomes transparent.

Add sauce ingredients and reserved juices, stir, and cook until sauce thickens.

Add bean sprouts and mandarin segments and toss to warm through.

Transfer to a hot platter and garnish with macadamia nuts and fresh coriander. Serve with rice and/or a tossed green salad.

Chicken teriyaki

Serves 6

600 g chicken fillet, skin and fat removed
2 teaspoons Ginger Paste (page 117)
2 medium shallots, peeled and finely diced
100 g snow peas, topped and tailed
100 g zucchini, sliced into thin rounds
100 g red capsicum, cut into thin strips
100 g baby corn, halved lengthwise
1 tablespoon cornflour
2 tablespoons water
slices of lemon

Sauce

2 tablespoons teriyaki sauce

1 cup freshly squeezed orange juice

1 tablespoon apple juice concentrate

¾ cup Chicken Stock (page 118) or water

Preparation

Season wok with canola oil.

Cut chicken into bite-size pieces and combine with ginger paste and shallots. Stand for thirty minutes.

Combine sauce ingredients.

Combine prepared vegetables.

Combine cornflour and water and mix together well.

Cooking

Stirfry chicken, ginger paste and shallots in a hot, dry wok for about two minutes or until chicken loses its raw exterior colour. Remove chicken from wok and keep warm.

Reduce heat, add half a cup of sauce to wok, stir, and cook until it begins to simmer.

Add vegetables and stirfry for about two minutes or until they are just tender and a vibrant colour.

➜

Combine cornflour mixture with remaining sauce and add to wok. Stir and cook until sauce thickens.

Add chicken and cook until it is warmed through.

Transfer to a hot platter and garnish with lemon slices. Serve with rice or couscous.

Tuscan chicken
with broccoli and carrot

Serves 4–6

2	cups Tuscan Tomato Sauce (page 117)
200 g	carrot, peeled and cut into chunks
200 g	broccoli, thinly sliced
1	cup Chicken Stock (page 118) or water
½	teaspoon Ginger Paste (page 117)
300 g	chicken fillet, skin and fat removed
1	teaspoon Garlic Paste (page 117)
1	onion, peeled and sliced into thin wedges
1	tablespoon finely chopped fresh coriander

Preparation

Season wok with canola oil.

Combine prepared vegetables.

Cut chicken into bite-size pieces and combine with garlic paste and onion.

Cooking

In a small saucepan heat tomato sauce to simmering point and keep warm.

Put vegetables and stock into a hot wok; cover and simmer for about two minutes or until vegetables are just tender and a vibrant colour.

Remove vegetables from wok and keep warm. Discard cooking liquid.

Season wok again with canola oil.

Stirfry chicken, garlic paste and onion in hot, dry wok for about two minutes or until chicken loses its raw exterior colour and onion becomes transparent.

Reduce heat and stir in sauce.

Add vegetables and coriander and cook until all ingredients are warmed through.

Transfer to a hot platter and serve with rice, rice noodles, a tossed green salad or toasted pita bread.

Chicken with corn and bean sprouts

Serves 4

600 g   chicken fillet, skin and fat removed
1   teaspoon Chilli, Ginger and Garlic Paste (page 117)
1   onion, peeled and finely diced
400 g   baby corn, halved lengthwise
200 g   bean sprouts
1   tablespoon cornflour
2   tablespoons water

Sauce
½ cup Chicken Stock (page 118) or water

1 tablespoon apple juice concentrate

1 tablespoon low-salt soy sauce

2 tablespoons mirin

Preparation

Season wok with canola oil.

Cut chicken into bite-size pieces and combine with chilli, ginger and garlic paste and onion.

Combine sauce ingredients.

Combine cornflour and water and mix together well.

Cooking

Stirfry chicken, paste and onion in a hot, dry wok for about two minutes or until chicken loses its raw exterior colour and onion becomes transparent.

Add corn and sauce, stir, and cook for about a minute.

Add cornflour mixture, stir, and cook until sauce thickens and glazes chicken and corn.

Add bean sprouts and toss through to warm.

Transfer to a hot platter and serve with rice or ribbon pasta.

Chilli chicken with snow peas

Serves 4

600 g	chicken fillet, skin and fat removed
1	tablespoon Chilli, Ginger and Garlic Paste (page 117)
250 g	snow peas, topped and tailed
250 g	bean sprouts
1	tablespoon cornflour
2	tablespoons water

Sauce

⅓ cup mirin

2 tablespoons apple juice concentrate

2 tablespoons low-salt soy sauce

½ cup Chicken Stock (page 118) or water

Preparation

Season wok with canola oil.

Cut chicken into bite-size pieces and combine with chilli, ginger and garlic paste.

Combine sauce ingredients.

Combine cornflour and water and mix together well.

Cooking

Stirfry chicken and paste in a hot, dry wok for about two minutes or until chicken loses its raw exterior colour.

Add snow peas and stirfry for about a minute.

Stir in sauce, cover, and cook for about a minute.

Add cornflour mixture, stir, and cook for about a minute or until sauce thickens.

Add bean sprouts and toss to warm through.

Transfer to a hot platter and serve with rice or noodles.

Chicken and basil curry

Serves 4

600 g chicken fillet, skin and fat removed
2 shallots, peeled and finely diced
2 teaspoons Vindaloo curry paste
¼ cup chopped fresh basil
1 cup grated carrot
1 tablespoon cornflour
1 × 375 mL can light evaporated milk (or soymilk)

Preparation

Season wok with canola oil and garlic clove.

Cut chicken into bite-size pieces and combine with shallots, curry paste, basil and grated carrot. Toss together and stand for thirty minutes. Drain juices and reserve.

Combine cornflour and milk and mix together well.

Cooking

Stirfry chicken mixture in a hot, dry wok for about two minutes or until it loses its raw exterior colour.

Add cornflour mixture and reserved juice; stir, and cook for about a minute or until sauce thickens and glazes chicken.

Transfer to a hot platter and serve with rice, fresh avocado slices and lightly toasted pita bread, or fresh pineapple slices and low-fat yoghurt.

Moroccan chicken and mango salad

Serves 4

500 g	chicken fillet, skin and fat removed
2	tablespoons ground coriander
1	tablespoon dried parsley flakes
2	teaspoons cumin
1	teaspoon turmeric
½	teaspoon chilli powder
1	teaspoon dried mint flakes
2	mangoes, peeled
½	cucumber, peeled, seeded and cut into half-rounds
300 g	mixed lettuce
1	cup low-fat yoghurt

Preparation

Season wok with canola oil.

Cut chicken into bite-size pieces and coat well with the combined spices. Leave to stand for about two hours.

Cut mango flesh into bite-size pieces.

Cooking

Stirfry chicken in a hot, dry wok for about three minutes or until it loses its raw exterior colour.

Remove wok from heat and add mango and cucumber. Toss lightly.

Serve on individual beds of crisp mixed lettuce and top with low-fat yoghurt.

Green chicken curry

Serves 4–6

400 g   chicken fillet, skin and fat removed
200 g   French beans, topped, tailed and halved
1½   tablespoons cornflour
1   cup light evaporated skim milk (or soymilk)
250 g   bean sprouts
         sprigs of fresh basil

Green curry paste

1 red Spanish onion, peeled and chopped

2 teaspoons Ginger Paste (page 117)

2 green chillies, seeded and chopped

¼ cup chopped fresh coriander

¼ cup chopped fresh lemon grass

1 teaspoon grated lemon rind

Preparation

Season wok with canola oil and garlic clove.

Cut chicken into bite-size pieces.

Combine green curry paste ingredients in a blender and process until almost smooth.

Combine cornflour and milk and mix together well.

Cooking

Add chicken to a hot, dry wok and stirfry for about two minutes or until it loses its raw exterior colour. Remove chicken from wok and keep warm.

Reduce heat, add green curry paste, stir, and cook constantly for about two minutes.

Add beans and stirfry for about two minutes or until beans become just tender and a vibrant green colour.

Add cornflour mixture, stir and cook until sauce thickens.

Add bean sprouts and toss to warm through.

Transfer to a hot platter and garnish with fresh basil. Serve with rice and/or a tossed green salad.

Moroccan chicken
with asparagus and beans

Serves 4

400 g	chicken fillet, skin and fat removed
2	tablespoons ground coriander
1	tablespoon dried parsley flakes
2	teaspoons cumin
1	teaspoon turmeric
½	teaspoon chilli powder
1	teaspoon dried mint flakes
200 g	asparagus spears, diagonally sliced
200 g	French beans, topped, tailed and halved
2	tablespoons cornflour
¾	cup Chicken Stock (page 118) or water

Preparation

Season wok with canola oil.

Cut chicken into bite-size pieces and coat well with combined spices. Leave chicken to stand for about two hours.

Combine prepared vegetables.

Combine cornflour and stock and mix together well.

Cooking

Stirfry chicken in a hot, dry wok for about three minutes or until it loses its raw exterior colour. Remove from wok and keep warm.

Add vegetables and stock and stirfry until vegetables are just tender and a vibrant colour.

Add cornflour mixture, stir and cook until sauce thickens.

Add chicken and cook until it is warmed through.

Transfer to a hot platter and serve with rice.

Red curry chicken
with almonds

Serves 4

400 g   chicken fillet, skin and fat removed
2   tablespoons red curry paste
1   teaspoon Ginger Paste (page 117)
60 g   blanched almonds
3   spring onions, diagonally sliced

Preparation

Season wok with canola oil.

Cut chicken into bite-size pieces and combine with red curry paste and ginger paste. Leave chicken to stand for about two hours before cooking.

Cooking

Put almonds into a moderately hot, dry wok and stirfry until golden brown. Set aside.

Add chicken and pastes to a hot, dry wok and stirfry for about three minutes or until chicken loses its raw exterior colour.

Add almonds and spring onions and stirfry to heat through.

Transfer to a hot platter and serve with rice.

Sticky ginger chicken

Serves 6

800 g chicken fillet, skin and fat removed

Sauce

2 shallots, finely chopped

1 tablespoon Ginger Paste (page 117)

1 teaspoon Vindaloo curry paste

2 tablespoons sugar-free marmalade jam

⅓ cup freshly squeezed orange juice

1 cup Chicken Stock (page 118) or water

1 tablespoon cornflour

Preparation

Season wok with canola oil.

Cut chicken into bite-size pieces.

Combine sauce ingredients and mix together well.

Cooking

Stirfry chicken in a hot, dry wok for about two minutes or until it loses its raw exterior colour.

Reduce heat, add sauce, stir, and cook for about two minutes or until sauce thickens and glazes chicken pieces.

Transfer to a hot platter and serve with rice, par-cooked vegetables (carrot and broccoli, for example) or a tossed green salad.

ſSicilian chicken

Serves 4–6

1	eggplant, washed and cut into bite-size cubes
1	teaspoon salt
1	red capsicum, seeded and cut into bite-size pieces
100 g	celery, sliced
1	cup Chicken Stock (page 118) or water
400 g	chicken fillet, skin and fat removed
1	teaspoon Garlic Paste (page 117)
1	onion, peeled and cut into thin wedges
2	cups Basilica Tomato Sauce (page 116)
20 g	olives, stoned and diced
1	tablespoon capers

Preparation

Season wok with canola oil.

Place eggplant and salt in a bowl, cover with water and stand for one hour. Drain and rinse under cold water to remove bitter juices.

Combine prepared capsicum and celery.

Cut chicken into bite-size pieces and combine with garlic paste and onion.

Combine olives and capers.

Cooking

Put eggplant, capsicum and celery with chicken stock into a hot wok. Cover and simmer until all vegetables are very soft and cooking liquid has been absorbed. Lift lid occasionally and stir so that vegetables do not stick. Remove vegetables from wok and keep warm.

Wipe out wok and season again with canola oil.

Stirfry chicken, garlic paste and onion in hot, dry wok for about two minutes or until chicken loses its raw exterior colour and onion becomes transparent.

Reduce heat, add tomato sauce, stir, and cook quickly so that sauce does not stick.

Reduce heat and add vegetables, olives and capers to wok Cook for about a minute.

Transfer to a hot platter and serve with rice and/or a tossed green salad.

Coconut tandoori chicken

Serves 4

600 g   chicken fillet, skin and fat removed
½   teaspoon Garlic Paste (page 117)
6   spring onions, finely sliced
200 g   baby corn, halved lengthwise
200 g   red capsicum, cut into chunks
200 g   snow peas, topped and tailed

Sauce

¾ cup Chicken Stock (page 118) or water

½ cup light coconut milk

2 tablespoons tandoori paste

1 tablespoon cornflour

Preparation

Season wok with canola oil.

Cut chicken into bite-size pieces and combine with garlic paste.

Combine sauce ingredients and mix together well.

Combine prepared vegetables.

Cooking

Stirfry chicken and garlic paste in a hot, dry wok for about two minutes or until chicken loses its raw exterior colour.

Add sauce, stir, and cook for about a minute or until sauce thickens.

While you are cooking chicken in wok, boil, microwave or steam vegetables until they are just tender and a vibrant colour.

Transfer chicken to a hot serving bowl and vegetables to a separate hot platter. Serve with rice.

Wok chicken cacciatore

Serves 4–6

600 g chicken fillet, skin and fat removed
1 teaspoon Garlic Paste (page 117)
1 onion, peeled and cut into thin wedges
½ cup dry white wine
1 tablespoon wine vinegar
2 cups Basilica Tomato Sauce (page 116)
50 g black olives
2 tablespoons chopped fresh parsley

Preparation

Season wok with canola oil.

Cut chicken into large bite-size pieces and combine with garlic paste and onion.

Combine wine and vinegar.

Cooking

Stirfry chicken, garlic paste and onion in a hot, dry wok for about two minutes or until chicken loses its raw exterior colour and onion becomes transparent.

Add wine and vinegar and stirfry for about a minute.

Reduce heat, add tomato sauce, stir and cook for about a minute.

Add olives and parsley and cook until all ingredients are warmed through.

Transfer to a hot platter and serve with rice and/or a tossed green salad.

Prawns with broccoli, celery and water chestnuts

Serves 4

1	cup Fish Stock or Chicken Stock (both page 118) or water
1	teaspoon Ginger Paste (page 117)
200 g	broccoli florets
200 g	celery, diagonally sliced
200 g	prawns, washed, peeled (but with tails left on) and deveined
1	× 230 g can water chestnuts, drained
2	tablespoons cornflour
1	extra cup stock or water
2	teaspoons finely chopped fresh coriander (optional)

Preparation

Season wok with canola oil.

Combine prepared vegetables.

Combine cornflour and extra stock or water and mix together well.

Cooking

Put stock, ginger paste and vegetables into a hot wok; cover, and simmer for about a minute or until vegetables are just tender and a vibrant colour.

Add prawns and water chestnuts and lightly stirfry for about a minute.

Add cornflour mixture, stir and cook until sauce thickens.

Transfer to a hot platter and sprinkle fresh coriander over the top. Serve with rice or rice noodles.

Scallops
with broccoli and zucchini

Serves 4

- ½ cup Fish Stock or Chicken Stock (both page 118) or water
- 1 teaspoon Ginger Paste (page 117)
- 250 g broccoli florets
- 250 g zucchini, cut into thin half-rounds
- 400 g scallops, washed and deveined
- 1 teaspoon finely chopped fresh dill

Sauce
⅔ cup light evaporated skim milk

⅓ cup light coconut milk

1 teaspoon red curry paste

2 tablespoons cornflour

Preparation

Season wok with canola oil.

Combine prepared vegetables.

Combine all sauce ingredients and mix together well.

Cooking

Put stock, ginger paste and vegetables into a hot wok; cover, and simmer for about a minute or until vegetables are just tender and a vibrant colour.

Use a slotted spoon to remove vegetables and keep warm.

Add sauce ingredients to wok, stir and cook until sauce thickens slightly.

Add scallops and lightly stirfry for about a minute.

Return vegetables to wok and cook until vegetables are warmed through.

Transfer to a hot platter and sprinkle fresh dill over the top. Serve with rice or pasta.

Opposite
Warm salmon and snow pea salad (page 34).

Braised scallops with vegetables

Serves 4

50 g	dried mushrooms
2	small shallots, peeled and finely diced
2	teaspoons Ginger Paste (page 117)
¼	cup Chicken Stock (page 118) or water
200 g	sugar peas, topped and tailed
100 g	broccoli, thinly sliced
200 g	baby corn
200 g	celery, diagonally sliced
400 g	scallops, washed and deveined
125 g	bean sprouts

Sauce

1 cup Chicken Stock (page 118)

1 tablespoon low-salt soy sauce

1 tablespoon dry sherry

1 tablespoon apple juice concentrate

1 tablespoon cornflour

Preparation

Season wok with canola oil.

Cover mushrooms with boiling water. Stand for about fifteen minutes or until mushrooms are soft. Drain and slice thinly.

Combine shallots, ginger paste and chicken stock. Combine prepared vegetables. Combine sauce ingredients and mix together well.

Cooking

Put shallots, ginger paste, stock and prepared vegetables into a hot wok and stirfry for about two minutes or until vegetables are tender and a vibrant colour.

Add sauce ingredients, stir, and cook until sauce just begins to thicken. Add scallops and mushrooms and cook for about two minutes or until scallops change colour. Add bean sprouts and stirfry for about a minute or until they are warmed through.

Transfer to a hot platter and serve with rice and/or a tossed green salad.

Opposite
Beef and capsicum (page 36).

Calamari and greens in marinara sauce

Serves 4–6

1	quantity Marinara Tomato Sauce (page 116)
600 g	calamari rings thinly sliced
½	cup Chicken Stock (page 118) or water
100 g	broccoli, thinly sliced
150 g	sugar peas, topped and tailed
150 g	zucchini, topped, tailed and cut into julienne strips
100 g	celery, diagonally sliced
1	tablespoon finely chopped fresh basil
	black pepper

Preparation

Season wok with canola oil.

Combine prepared vegetables.

Cooking

Heat tomato sauce and keep warm.

Add calamari rings to a saucepan of rapidly boiling water. Use a slotted spoon to remove calamari after about thirty seconds. Rinse under cold water and set aside.

Put chicken stock and vegetables into a hot wok and stirfry for about two minutes or until vegetables are just tender and a vibrant green.

Reduce heat, stir in tomato sauce and bring to simmering point.

Add calamari, fresh basil and black pepper to taste; stir and cook a further minute or until calamari is warmed through.

Transfer to a hot platter and serve with pasta and/or a tossed salad.

Scallops
in creamy basil sauce

Serves 4

1	cup Fish Stock or Chicken Stock (both page 118) or water
125 g	sugar peas, topped and tailed
100 g	green capsicum, seeded and cut into julienne strips
100 g	red capsicum, seeded and cut into julienne strips
100 g	carrot, cut into julienne strips
100 g	zucchini, cut into julienne strips
400 g	scallops, washed and deveined
1	tablespoon finely chopped fresh basil
	black pepper

Sauce
¾ cup light evaporated skim milk

2½ tablespoons cornflour

2 tablespoons water

Preparation

Season wok with canola oil.

Combine prepared vegetables.

Combine sauce ingredients and mix together well.

Cooking

Put stock and vegetables into a hot wok; cover, and simmer for about a minute or until vegetables are just tender and a vibrant colour. Use a slotted spoon to remove vegetables and keep warm.

Reduce heat and add sauce ingredients; stir and cook until sauce thickens slightly.

Add scallops and lightly stirfry for about a minute.

Add fresh basil and pepper to taste.

Return vegetables to wok and stirfry until vegetables are warmed through.

Transfer to a hot platter and serve with rice or pasta.

Seafood in mustard sauce

Serves 4–6

1 teaspoon Garlic Paste (page 117)
1 onion, peeled and sliced
¼ cup dry white wine
250 g French beans, topped, tailed and halved
600 g seafood, including prawns, scallops, fish pieces, calamari, mussels etc.
1 tablespoon finely chopped chives

Sauce
1 cup low-fat milk or soymilk

2 teaspoons wholegrain mustard

½ teaspoon hot English mustard

1 tablespoon cornflour

Preparation

Season wok with canola oil.

Combine garlic paste, onion and dry white wine.

Combine sauce ingredients and mix together well.

Prepare seafood by shelling, cleaning etc.

Cooking

Put garlic paste, onion and wine into a hot wok with beans and stirfry until beans are just tender and a vibrant green.

Reduce heat and add sauce ingredients; stir and cook until sauce just begins to thicken.

Add seafood, cover, and cook for about three minutes or until fish changes colour and is tender.

Transfer to a hot platter and sprinkle with chives. Serve with rice, pasta or steamed vegetables (pumpkin and sweet potato, for example).

Sea perch
with zucchini in orange sauce

Serves 4–6

¼ cup Chicken Stock (page 118) or water
1 onion, peeled and sliced
200 g zucchini, topped, tailed and cut into rounds
600 g sea perch, cut into bite-size pieces

Sauce

¼ cup apple juice concentrate

2 teaspoons Ginger Paste (page 117)

1 cup freshly squeezed orange juice

¾ cup dry sherry

1 tablespoon low-salt soy sauce

1 tablespoon grated orange rind

2 tablespoons cornflour

Preparation

Season wok with canola oil.

Combine onion and zucchini.

Combine sauce ingredients and mix together well.

Cooking

Put stock, onion and zucchini into a hot wok and stirfry for about two minutes or until vegetables are just tender and a vibrant colour.

Add sauce ingredients, stir, and cook until just thickened.

Reduce heat and add sea perch. Cook a further three minutes or until fish is tender.

Transfer to a hot platter and serve with rice, couscous or pasta.

Bok choy tuna

Serves 4–6

600 g	bok choy, roughly chopped
1	medium Spanish onion, peeled and diced
1	× 425 g can salt-free tuna, well drained
200 g	bean sprouts
1	tablespoon cornflour
2	tablespoons water
	black pepper
100 g	cooked pasta (penne, ribbon, shell or soyaroni)
3	sprigs of Italian parsley

Sauce

1 tablespoon Ginger Paste (page 117)

1 teaspoon dried basil

½ teaspoon ground oregano

1 tablespoon lemon juice

1 tablespoon grated lemon rind

3 tablespoons teriyaki sauce

1 cup Fish Stock (page 118) or water

Preparation

Season wok with canola oil.

Combine sauce ingredients.

Combine bok choy and onion.

Combine tuna and bean sprouts.

Combine cornflour and water and mix together well.

Cooking

Put sauce ingredients into a hot wok. When sauce begins to simmer add bok choy and onion and stirfry for about two minutes or until vegetables are just tender and a vibrant colour.

Add tuna and bean sprouts and continue to stirfry until tuna is warmed through.

Add cornflour mixture, stir, and cook for about a minute or until sauce thickens. Season with black pepper to taste.

Add cooked pasta and stirfry to mix ingredients evenly and to warm. Transfer to a hot serving platter and garnish with Italian parsley.

Tuna and mushroom pasta

Serves 4–6

250 g	fettuccine
1	onion, peeled and finely diced
100 g	celery, finely diced
200 g	mushrooms, washed and thinly sliced
⅓	cup Vegetable Stock or Chicken Stock (both page 118) or water
2	cups Basilica Tomato Sauce (page 116)
1	× 425 g can salt-free tuna, drained
2	tablespoons finely chopped chives
	black pepper
	sprigs of Italian parsley

Preparation

Season wok with canola oil.

Combine prepared vegetables.

Cooking

Cook fettuccine in boiling water until al dente. Drain and keep warm.

Put vegetables and stock into a hot wok and stirfry for about two minutes or until vegetables are just tender and cooking liquid absorbed.

Reduce heat, add tomato sauce and stirfry quickly for about a minute.

Add tuna and continue to stirfry for about two minutes or until it is warmed through.

Add chives and season with black pepper to taste.

Add cooked pasta and stirfry to mix evenly and warm all ingredients.

Transfer to a hot serving platter and garnish with Italian parsley.

Warm salmon
and snow pea salad

Serves 4

1	teaspoon Ginger Paste (page 117)
2	tablespoons low-salt soy sauce
1	tablespoon dry sherry
1	tablespoon apple juice concentrate
250 g	snow peas, topped and tailed
650 g	fresh salmon, cut into bite-size pieces
1	teaspoon cornflour
2	tablespoons water
2	teaspoons freshly chopped dill
100 g	mixed lettuce leaves, washed

Preparation

Season wok with canola oil.

Combine ginger paste, soy sauce, sherry and apple juice concentrate.

Combine cornflour and water and mix together well.

Cooking

Put ginger paste, soy sauce, sherry and apple juice concentrate into hot wok and heat to just simmering.

Add snow peas and stirfry for about a minute or until they turn a vibrant green colour.

Add salmon, cover, and gently cook for about a minute or until salmon loses its raw exterior colour and becomes tender.

Add cornflour mixture, stir gently and cook until sauce thickens.

Add dill. To serve, place lettuce on four individual plates. Spoon salmon and snow peas evenly over the lettuce.

New ways with meat

Use the best cuts of lean meat, sliced thinly, and combine them with flavoursome stocks, spices, herbs and a wide variety of crisp vegetables.

Beef and capsicum

Serves 6

500 g lean beef fillet
1 onion, peeled and sliced
½ teaspoon Garlic Paste (page 117)
1 green capsicum, cut into strips
1 red capsicum, cut into strips
1 yellow capsicum, cut into strips
¼ cup Beef Stock (page 118) or water

Sauce

1 teaspoon Ginger Paste (page 117)

1 tablespoon tomato paste

1 tablespoon low-salt soy sauce

½ teaspoon dried basil

½ teaspoon dried oregano

1 cup Beef Stock (page 118) or water

1 tablespoon cornflour

Preparation

Season wok with canola oil.

Cut beef into bite-size strips and combine with onion and garlic paste.

Combine prepared capsicum.

Combine sauce ingredients.

Cooking

Stirfry beef, onion and garlic paste in a hot, dry wok for about two minutes or until beef loses its raw exterior colour.

Reduce heat, add capsicum and stock and continue to stirfry until capsicum is just tender and a vibrant colour.

Add sauce ingredients and simmer for about three minutes or until sauce thickens.

Transfer to a hot platter and serve with rice and/or a tossed green salad.

Neapolitan beef

Serves 4

200 g asparagus spears, diagonally sliced
4 baby bok choy, washed and cut in half
½ cup Beef Stock (page 118) or water
400 g lean beef fillet
2 cups Neapolitan Tomato Sauce (page 116)
2 tablespoons roughly chopped fresh parsley
black pepper

Preparation

Season wok with canola oil.

Cut beef into thin slices.

Combine asparagus and bok choy.

Cooking

Put asparagus, bok choy and beef stock into a hot wok and stirfry for about a minute or until asparagus and bok choy are just tender and a vibrant green. Set aside and keep warm.

Wipe out wok and season again with canola oil.

Stirfry beef in hot, dry wok for about two minutes or until it loses its raw exterior colour.

Reduce heat, add tomato sauce, stir, and cook quickly so that sauce does not stick.

Add vegetables and stirfry for about a minute or until they are warmed through.

Add fresh parsley and black pepper to taste. Serve with rice and/or a tossed green salad.

Black-bean beef
with bamboo shoots

Serves 4

400 g lean beef fillet
1 green chilli, including seeds, finely minced
1 onion, peeled and sliced
1 teaspoon Ginger Paste (page 117)
1 tablespoon dry sherry
1 teaspoon curry powder
1 tablespoon black-bean sauce
200 g broccoli, cut into florets
1 × 230 g can bamboo shoots, drained and thinly sliced
1 cup Beef Stock (page 118) or water
2 tablespoons cornflour
2 tablespoons water

Preparation
Season wok with canola oil.

Cut beef into thin slices and combine with chilli, onion, ginger paste, sherry, curry powder and black-bean sauce. Allow to stand for at least thirty minutes.

Combine broccoli and bamboo shoots.

Combine cornflour and water and mix well.

Cooking
Drain juices from beef and reserve. Stirfry beef mixture in a hot, dry wok for about two minutes or until beef loses its raw exterior.

Add broccoli, bamboo shoots, beef stock and reserved juices, and stirfry for about a minute or until broccoli becomes just tender and a vibrant green.

Add cornflour mixture, stir, and cook until sauce thickens and glazes beef and broccoli. Serve with rice.

Black-bean beef
with cabbage

Serves 4

500 g	lean beef fillet
1	tablespoon Ginger Paste (page 117)
1	green chilli, including seeds, finely minced
1	tablespoon black-bean sauce
1	onion, peeled and sliced into wedges
200 g	cabbage, roughly chopped
100 g	spring onions, diagonally sliced
1	cup Beef Stock (page 118) or water
2	tablespoons cornflour
2	tablespoons water

Preparation

Season wok with canola oil.

Cut beef into thin slices and combine with ginger paste, chilli, black-bean sauce and onion. Allow to stand for at least two hours.

Combine cabbage and spring onions.

Combine cornflour and water and mix well.

Cooking

Drain juices from beef and reserve. Stirfry beef mixture in a hot, dry wok for about two minutes or until beef loses its raw exterior colour.

Reduce heat and add cabbage, spring onions, beef stock and reserved meat juices. Stirfry for about a minute or until the cabbage becomes just tender and a vibrant green.

Add cornflour mixture, stir, and cook until sauce thickens and glazes beef and cabbage.

Transfer to a hot platter and serve with noodles.

Beef chow mein

Serves 4

250 g thin spaghetti
400 g lean beef fillet
1 tablespoon sweet chilli sauce
2 tablespoons low-salt soy sauce
1 tablespoon dry sherry
1 onion, peeled and sliced
125 g celery, diagonally sliced
125 g red capsicum, seeded and sliced
125 g broccoli florets
125 g mushrooms, thinly sliced
1 cup Beef Stock (page 118) or water
1 tablespoon cornflour
2 tablespoons water
125 g bean sprouts

Preparation

Season wok with canola oil.

Cut beef into thin strips and dice finely.

Combine beef with chilli sauce, soy sauce and sherry, and marinate for at least two hours.

Combine all vegetables except bean sprouts.

Combine cornflour and water and mix together well.

Cooking

Cook spaghetti until al dente; drain and keep warm.

Stirfry beef in a hot, dry wok for about two minutes or until it loses its raw exterior colour. Remove from wok and keep warm.

Add vegetables and stock, cover, and simmer for about a minute or until vegetables are just tender and a vibrant colour.

Add cornflour mixture, stir, and cook until sauce thickens slightly.

Return beef to wok and stirfry until it is warmed through.

Add bean sprouts and lightly stirfry to combine.

Arrange spaghetti on a hot serving platter and top with the beef chow mein.

Aromatic Chinese beef
with apple

Serves 4

500 g lean beef fillet
1 large onion, peeled and sliced
2 large Granny Smith apples, peeled and cut into eight
        wedges each
2 teaspoons five-spice powder
2 teaspoons Ginger Paste (page 117)
2 tablespoons low-salt soy sauce
1 tablespoon hoi sin sauce
2 tablespoons cornflour
1 cup Beef Stock (page 118) or water

Preparation
Season wok with canola oil.

Cut beef into thin slices and combine with onion, apple,
five-spice powder, ginger paste, soy sauce and hoi sin sauce;
allow to stand for about two hours.

Combine cornflour and beef stock and mix together well.

Cooking
Stirfry beef, onion and apple mixture in a hot, dry wok in three
different lots, until beef loses its raw exterior colour. Remove
each batch from wok as it is cooked, and keep warm.

Add cornflour mixture to wok; stir, and cook for about a minute
or until sauce thickens.

Return beef, onion and apple to wok and cook until warmed
through.

Transfer to a hot platter and serve with rice.

Curried beef with snow peas

Serves 4

500 g	lean beef fillet
1	onion, peeled and sliced
2	teaspoons Ginger Paste (page 117)
1	teaspoon Vindaloo curry paste
1	teaspoon coriander paste
1	teaspoon turmeric
200 g	carrots, cut into julienne strips
150 g	snow peas, topped, tailed and cut into julienne strips
1	cup Beef Stock (page 118) or water
1	tablespoon cornflour
¼	cup water
¼	cup chopped fresh coriander

Preparation

Season wok with canola oil.

Cut beef into thin slices and combine with onion, ginger paste, curry paste, coriander paste and turmeric; marinate for at least two hours.

Combine carrots and snow peas.

Combine cornflour and water and mix together well.

Cooking

Stirfry beef and onion mixture in a hot, dry wok for about two minutes or until beef loses its raw exterior colour.

Remove beef and onions from wok and keep warm.

Add carrots, snow peas and beef stock; cover, and simmer for about a minute or until vegetables are just tender and a vibrant colour.

Add cornflour mixture, stir and cook until sauce thickens slightly.

Return beef and onions to wok and stirfry until beef is warmed through.

Transfer to a hot platter and garnish with fresh coriander. Serve with rice and/or a tossed green salad.

Creamy beef and mushroom pasta

Serves 6

250 g ribbon pasta
400 g lean beef fillet
  1 teaspoon Ginger Paste (page 117)
  1 large onion, peeled and sliced
400 g mushrooms, cut in half
  ¼ cup Beef Stock (page 118) or water
  2 tablespoons cornflour
  1 × 375 mL can light evaporated skim milk
  1 teaspoon dried basil
  1 cup finely chopped spring onion

Preparation

Season wok with canola oil.

Cut beef into thin slices and combine with ginger paste.

Combine onion and mushrooms. Combine cornflour, evaporated milk and basil and mix together well.

Cooking

Cook ribbon pasta in boiling water until al dente. Drain and keep warm.

Stirfry beef in a hot, dry wok until it loses its raw exterior colour. Remove from wok and keep warm.

Add onion, mushrooms and beef stock; cover, and simmer for about two minutes or until mushrooms are softened. Reduce heat, stir in cornflour mixture, and cook until sauce thickens slightly.

Return beef to wok. Fold in pasta and spring onions; stirfry until pasta and beef are warmed through.

Transfer to a hot platter and serve with a tossed green salad.

Honey and soy beef with mushrooms

Serves 4

500 g	lean beef fillet
1	tablespoon Ginger Paste (page 117)
2	tablespoons low-salt soy sauce
1	tablespoon honey
300 g	mushrooms, halved
250 g	broccoli, cut into florets
1	cup Beef Stock (page 118) or water
2	tablespoons cornflour
¼	cup water
2	spring onions, diagonally sliced

Preparation

Season wok with canola oil.

Cut beef into thin slices, combine with ginger paste, soy sauce and honey, and allow to stand for at least two hours.

Combine mushrooms and broccoli.

Combine cornflour and water and mix together well.

Cooking

Stirfry beef mixture in a hot, dry wok for about two minutes or until beef loses its raw exterior colour. Remove beef from wok and keep warm.

Add mushrooms, broccoli and beef stock to wok; cover, and simmer for about two minutes or until vegetables are soft.

Add cornflour mixture, stir and cook until sauce thickens slightly.

Return beef to wok and stirfry until it is warmed through.

Transfer to a hot platter and garnish with spring onions. Serve with rice and/or a tossed green salad.

Lonsdale coriander beef

Serves 4

500 g lean beef fillet
1 teaspoon Garlic Paste (page 117)
2 spring onions, diagonally sliced

Sauce

1 teaspoon Ginger
Paste (page 117)

1 teaspoon Chilli,
Ginger and Garlic
Paste (page 117)

1 spring onion,
finely chopped

1 tablespoon
coriander paste

¼ cup light
coconut milk

1 teaspoon
cornflour

¼ cup water

Preparation

Season wok with canola oil.

Cut beef into thin strips and combine with garlic paste.

Combine sauce ingredients.

Cooking

Stirfry beef in a hot, dry wok for about two minutes or until it loses its raw exterior colour. Remove beef from wok and keep warm.

Reduce heat, add sauce ingredients, stir, and cook for about two minutes or until sauce thickens.

Return beef to wok and stirfry until it is warmed through.

Transfer to a hot platter and garnish with spring onions. Serve with rice and/or a mixed lettuce salad.

Beef mediterranean

Serves 4

1   onion, peeled and finely diced
1   red capsicum, seeded and finely diced
10 black olives, stoned and minced
1   teaspoon dried basil
500 g lean minced beef
1   tablespoon balsamic vinegar

Preparation

Season wok with canola oil.

Combine onion, capsicum, olives, basil and beef.

Cooking

Add onion, capsicum, olives, basil and beef to a moderately hot, dry wok and stirfry for about four minutes or until beef loses its raw exterior colour.

Stir in balsamic vinegar at the very last minute before serving with rice or pasta.

Sherry beef
with bamboo shoots

Serves 4

500 g	lean beef fillet
½	teaspoon Garlic Paste (page 117)
2	teaspoons Ginger Paste (page 117)
1	onion, peeled and sliced
2	tablespoons dry sherry
1	tablespoon low-salt soy sauce
2	teaspoons finely grated orange rind
1	× 230 g can bamboo shoots, drained and thinly sliced
200 g	celery, diagonally sliced
½	cup Beef Stock (page 118) or water
1	teaspoon cornflour
¼	cup water
2	small red chillies

Preparation

Season wok with canola oil.

Cut beef into thin slices and combine with garlic paste, ginger paste, onion, sherry, soy sauce and orange rind. Marinate for at least two hours.

Combine bamboo shoots and celery.

Combine cornflour and water and mix together well.

Cut chillies in half and remove seeds. Cut into long thin strips and place in a bowl of very cold water.

Cooking

Stirfry beef and onion mixture in a hot, dry wok until beef loses its raw exterior colour. Remove beef and onions from wok and keep warm.

Add bamboo shoots, celery and beef stock to wok. Cover, and simmer for about a minute or until celery is just tender and a vibrant colour.

Add cornflour mixture, stir and cook until sauce thickens slightly.

Return beef and onions to wok and stirfry until beef is warmed through.

Transfer to a hot platter and garnish with thin strips of curled red chilli. Serve with rice and/or a tossed green salad.

Spicy lamb with rice

Serves 4–6

600 g   lean minced lamb

2   medium onions, peeled and finely diced

1   tablespoon Ginger Paste (page 117)

1   teaspoon coriander

1   teaspoon cumin

1   small green capsicum, seeded and finely chopped

1   small yellow capsicum, seeded and finely chopped

1   small red capsicum, seeded and finely chopped

2   carrots, finely chopped

1   small eggplant, finely chopped

1   cup sultanas

1   cup Vegetable Stock (page 118) or water

1   cup cooked brown rice

Preparation

Season wok with canola oil and garlic clove.

Combine lamb, onion, ginger paste, coriander and cumin.

Combine prepared vegetables.

Cooking

Stirfry lamb mixture in a hot, dry wok for about three minutes or until meat loses its raw exterior colour.

Reduce heat, add vegetables, sultanas and stock to wok, and stirfry for about four minutes or until vegetables are just tender, sultanas are plump and all moisture has been absorbed.

Add rice and continue to stirfry until it is warmed through.

Transfer to a hot platter and serve with cooked vegetables (pumpkin, sweet potato or broccoli, for example) or a tossed green salad.

Sweet and sour pork

500 g	lean pork
1	tablespoon cornflour
1	cup Chicken Stock (page 118) or water
200 g	red capsicum, cut into chunks
200 g	celery, diagonally cut
200 g	cucumber, seeds removed, cut into chunks
100 g	French beans, topped, tailed and diagonally cut
1	× 440 g can unsweetened pineapple pieces
2	tablespoons cornflour
2	tablespoons water

Sauce

2 tablespoons tomato paste

2 tablespoons low-salt soy sauce

¼ cup white wine vinegar

1 tablespoon dry sherry

¾ cup reserved unsweetened pineapple juice

Preparation

Season wok with canola oil.

Cut pork into bite-size pieces and toss in cornflour until all pork is well coated.

Combine prepared vegetables. Drain pineapple pieces and reserve juice.

Combine sauce ingredients. Combine cornflour and water and mix together well.

Cooking

Stirfry pork in a hot, dry wok for about three minutes or until pork loses its raw exterior colour. Remove pork from wok and keep warm.

Add chicken stock, vegetables and pineapple. Cover, and simmer for about three minutes or until vegetables are just tender and a vibrant colour. Add sauce ingredients and pork. Cover and simmer for about a minute. Add cornflour mixture, stir, and cook for a further minute or until sauce thickens and glazes pork and vegetables.

Transfer to a hot platter and serve with rice.

Plum pork
with bok choy

Serves 4

600 g	lean pork fillet, thinly sliced
2	teaspoons Ginger Paste (page 117)
2	tablespoons plum sauce
2	sticks celery, diagonally sliced
600 g	bok choy, roughly chopped
1	cup Chicken Stock (page 118) or water
1	tablespoon cornflour
¼	cup water

Preparation

Season wok with canola oil.

Combine pork, ginger paste and plum sauce, and marinate for thirty minutes.

Combine prepared vegetables.

Combine cornflour and water and mix together well.

Cooking

Drain pork and reserve juices.

Stirfry pork in a hot, dry wok for about three minutes or until it loses its raw exterior colour.

Add vegetables, chicken stock and reserved meat juices to wok. Cover, and cook vegetables for about two minutes or until they are just tender and a vibrant colour.

Add cornflour mixture, stir, and cook for about a minute or until sauce thickens and glazes pork and vegetables.

Transfer to a hot platter and serve on a bed of fresh bean sprouts or with rice.

Veal marsala

Serves 4–6

250 g fettuccine
500 g veal steaks, trimmed of fat
1 teaspoon Garlic Paste (page 117)
3 tablespoons marsala
sprigs of fresh thyme

Sauce

1 cup light evaporated skim milk

1 tablespoon capers

2 tablespoons finely chopped fresh parsley

1 tablespoon cornflour

black pepper

Preparation

Season wok with canola oil.

Cut veal into bite-size pieces and combine with garlic paste and marsala. Allow to stand for at least thirty minutes.

Combine sauce ingredients and mix together well.

Cooking

Cook fettuccine in boiling water. Drain and keep warm.

Drain veal and reserve juice.

Stirfry veal in a hot, dry wok for about a minute or until it loses its raw exterior colour.

Reduce heat, add reserved juices and sauce ingredients, and cook for about two minutes.

Add pasta and stirfry all ingredients until they are evenly mixed and pasta is warmed through.

Season with black pepper to taste.

Transfer to a hot platter and garnish with fresh thyme. Serve with a tossed green salad.

What's in season?

You don't have to be a vegetarian to relish meatless main courses, and fruit desserts are universally popular. Wok cooking helps to retain the nutritional value of all fresh seasonal produce.

Red-hot beans and eggplant

Serves 4–6

500 g	eggplant, roughly chopped
2	teaspoons salt
½	cup Chicken Stock (page 118)
1	Spanish onion, peeled and sliced
200 g	French beans, halved
1	red capsicum, seeded and cut into strips
2	shallots, peeled and diced

Sauce

1 teaspoon Ginger Paste (page 117)

1 teaspoon Garlic Paste (page 117)

1 tablespoon finely chopped fresh basil

2 tablespoons low-salt soy sauce

2 teaspoons sweet chilli sauce

1½ cups Chicken Stock (page 118)

1 teaspoon cornflour

Preparation

Season wok with canola oil.

Place eggplant and salt in a bowl, cover with water and stand for one hour. Drain and rinse under cold water to remove bitter juices. Drain well.

Combine onion, beans and capsicum.

Combine sauce ingredients and mix together well.

Cooking

Put eggplant and stock into a hot wok and stirfry for thirty seconds.

Add other vegetables and stirfry until vegetables are tender and a vibrant colour.

Add sauce, stir, and cook until sauce thickens.

Transfer to a hot platter, and serve with rice, pasta or a tossed green salad. Alternatively, make the dish an accompaniment to your main course.

Beans, broccoli and mushrooms in black-bean sauce

Serves 4–6

250 g fresh mixed mushrooms (such as cultivated, shiitake and oyster mushrooms, plus chanterelles)

2 tablespoons dry white wine

200 g French beans, topped, tailed and halved

250 g broccoli, cut into florets

Sauce

¾ cup Chicken Stock or Vegetable Stock (both page 118)

1 teaspoon Ginger Paste (page 117)

1 tablespoon black-bean sauce

½ teaspoon Vindaloo curry paste

1 tablespoon dry sherry

2 teaspoons cornflour

Preparation

Season wok with canola oil.

Chop mushrooms and put aside tough stems for stockpot.

Combine prepared beans and broccoli.

Combine all sauce ingredients and mix together well.

Cooking

Put mushrooms into a hot, dry wok and stirfry for about thirty seconds. Add wine and stirfry for a further two minutes.

Add beans and broccoli, then stir, cover and cook until vegetables are just tender and a vibrant green colour.

Add sauce ingredients, stir, and cook until sauce thickens.

Transfer to a hot platter, and serve with rice or noodles. Alternatively, make the dish an accompaniment to barbecued meats or fish.

Curried cauliflower
with peanuts

Serves 4–6

1 kg	cauliflower, cut into florets
½	cup Chicken Stock (page 118)
1	teaspoon finely chopped fresh coriander
200 g	carrot, chopped
½	onion, peeled and sliced
½	cup dry-roasted salt-free peanuts

Sauce

2 teaspoons Ginger Paste (page 117)

1 teaspoon Garlic Paste (page 117)

1 teaspoon tomato paste

1 teaspoon Vindaloo curry paste

1 teaspoon cornflour

1½ cups Chicken Stock (page 118) or water

Preparation

Season wok with canola oil.

Combine carrot and onion.

Combine sauce ingredients.

Cooking

Put cauliflower, chicken stock and coriander into a hot wok and stirfry until cauliflower is just tender and a vibrant colour. Remove cauliflower from wok and set aside.

While cauliflower is cooking in wok, boil, steam or microwave carrot and onion together until soft. Drain well. Place in a blender with sauce ingredients and purée until smooth.

Season wok again with canola oil.

Add puréed sauce to a moderately hot wok and cook until sauce thickens.

Add peanuts and cauliflower and cook until all ingredients are warmed through.

Transfer to a hot platter and serve with rice, noodles or a tossed green salad.

Opposite
Noodles with hot spicy pumpkin and peas (page 92).

Coriander cauliflower with pine nuts

Serves 4–6

600 g cauliflower, cut into florets
2 onions, peeled and cut into wedges
¼ cup Chicken Stock (page 118)
½ cup dry-roasted pine nuts

Sauce

1 teaspoon Ginger Paste (page 117)

1 teaspoon Chilli, Ginger and Garlic Paste (page 117)

1 spring onion, finely chopped

1 tablespoon coriander paste

¼ cup light coconut milk

2 teaspoons cornflour

¼ cup Chicken Stock (page 118)

2 tablespoons chopped chives

Preparation

Season wok with canola oil.

Combine cauliflower and onion.

Combine sauce ingredients and mix together well.

Cooking

Put cauliflower, onion and stock into a hot wok and stirfry until vegetables are tender and a vibrant colour.

Add sauce, stir, and cook until sauce thickens.

Transfer to a hot platter and garnish with pine nuts. Serve with rice or noodles. Alternatively, make the dish an accompaniment to barbecued meats or other main courses.

Opposite
Surfers vegetable soup (page 111).

Pumpkin and eggplant caponata

Serves 4–6

400 g eggplant, washed and cut into bite-size cubes
200 g pumpkin, peeled and cut into bite-size cubes
200 g red capsicum, seeded and cut into bite-size pieces
    2 onions, peeled and sliced into thin wedges
    2 cups Chicken Stock (page 118) or water
    1 teaspoon Ginger Paste (page 117)
    2 cups Basilica Tomato Sauce (page 116)
  20 g olives, stoned and diced
    1 tablespoon capers
       black pepper

Preparation

Combine prepared vegetables.

Combine chicken stock and ginger paste.

Combine olives and capers.

Cooking

Add vegetables and stock to a hot wok and stirfry until all vegetables are very soft and cooking liquid has been absorbed.

Reduce heat, add tomato sauce, stir, and cook for about a minute.

Add olives, capers and black pepper to taste and stirfry until all ingredients are warmed through.

Transfer to a hot platter and serve with rice, a tossed green salad or toasted pita bread.

Vegetables in creamy basil sauce

Serves 4

½	cup Vegetable Stock (page 118) or water
200 g	cauliflower, thinly sliced
150 g	broccoli, thinly sliced
100 g	asparagus spears, halved
100 g	yellow squash, thinly sliced
100 g	red capsicum, thinly sliced
1	teaspoon cumin
1	teaspoon turmeric
½	teaspoon garam masala
2	teaspoons Ginger Paste (page 117)
1	× 375 ml can light evaporated milk
1	tablespoon cornflour
½	cup water
1	tablespoon chopped fresh basil

Preparation

Season wok with canola oil and ginger.

Combine prepared vegetables.

Combine spices.

Combine cornflour and water and mix together well.

Cooking

Put stock into wok and heat until just simmering.

Add vegetables, cover, and cook for about three minutes or until vegetables are just tender and a vibrant colour.

Remove vegetables from wok and keep warm. Discard cooking stock.

Season wok again with canola oil.

Stirfry spices for about one minute on low heat, then add ginger paste and milk, stirring until mixture begins to bubble but not boil. Add cornflour mixture, stir, and cook until sauce boils and thickens.

Return vegetables to wok and toss them through the sauce.

Transfer to a hot platter and serve with rice or pasta.

Ginger wok greens and bamboo shoots

Serves 4–6

½ cup Chicken Stock (page 118)
1 tablespoon Ginger Paste (page 117)
1 teaspoon sweet chilli sauce
250 g asparagus spears, halved
200 g French beans, topped, tailed and halved
200 g cucumber, seeded and cut into julienne strips
200 g zucchini, topped and tailed, cut into julienne strips
500 g bok choy, washed and roughly chopped
1 × 230 g can bamboo shoots, drained well and sliced

Sauce

1 cup Chicken Stock (page 118)

1 tablespoon low-salt soy sauce

1 tablespoon cornflour

1 teaspoon finely chopped fresh coriander

Preparation

Season wok with canola oil.

Combine chicken stock, ginger paste and chilli sauce.

Combine prepared vegetables.

Combine sauce ingredients and mix together well.

Cooking

Put stock, ginger paste, chilli sauce and vegetables into a hot wok and stirfry for about a minute. Cover and cook for a further minute or until vegetables are just tender and a vibrant green colour.

Add bamboo shoots.

Add sauce ingredients, stir, and cook until thickened.

Transfer to a hot platter and sprinkle with coriander. Serve with rice, couscous or rice noodles.

Mushroom with baby bok choy

Serves 4

400 g mushrooms, thinly sliced
2 teaspoons Vindaloo curry paste
1 teaspoon turmeric
8 baby bok choy heads, thoroughly washed
1 tablespoon cornflour
2 tablespoons water

Sauce
1 tablespoon low-salt soy sauce

1 tablespoon apple juice concentrate

1 cup Vegetable Stock (page 118) or water

Preparation
Season wok with canola oil and garlic clove.

Combine mushrooms, curry paste and turmeric.

Combine sauce ingredients.

Combine cornflour and water and mix together well.

Cooking
Stirfry mushroom mixture in a moderately hot, dry wok for about a minute.

Add sauce ingredients, stir, and cook for a further two minutes.

Reduce heat, add bok choy, cover, and cook for about two minutes or until bok choy is tender and a vibrant colour.

Add cornflour mixture, stir, and cook for about a minute or until sauce boils and thickens.

Transfer to a hot platter and serve with rice or noodles.

$\int$ate mushrooms and onions

Serves 4–6

600 g mushrooms, washed and halved
   2 onions, peeled and sliced
   2 tablespoons finely chopped fresh chives

Sauce

½ teaspoon five-spice powder

¼ teaspoon chilli powder

4 tablespoons tahini paste

1 teaspoon curry powder

1 tablespoon low-salt soy sauce

1 teaspoon cornflour

¾ cup Chicken Stock (page 118) or water

Preparation

Season wok with canola oil.

Combine mushrooms and onions.

Combine sauce ingredients and mix together well.

Cooking

Stirfry mushrooms and onions in a hot, dry wok for about two minutes or until vegetables begin to soften.

Reduce heat, add sauce ingredients, stir, and cook until sauce thickens.

Add chives.

Transfer to a hot platter and serve with rice or noodles. Alternatively, make the dish an accompaniment to barbecued meats or other main courses.

Potato and pea curry

Serves 4

800 g new potatoes, cut into bite-size pieces
2 cups Vegetable Stock or Chicken Stock (both page 118)
100 g red capsicum, seeded and diced
100 g fresh or frozen peas
2 spring onions, diagonally sliced

Sauce
1 tablespoon red curry paste

½ teaspoon turmeric

⅓ cup light coconut milk

Preparation
Season wok with canola oil.

Combine sauce ingredients.

Cooking
Add potatoes and stock to a moderately hot wok and stirfry for about four minutes or until potatoes are just tender. The cooking liquid will reduce and thicken during cooking.

Add sauce ingredients, capsicum and peas and continue to stirfry until vegetables are tender.

Transfer to a hot platter and garnish with spring onions. Serve with rice, fish or chicken.

*S*esame parsnip and *S*carrot in sherry sauce

Serves 4–6

400 g	parsnip, cut into thick chips
350 g	carrot, cut into thick chips
¼	cup Chicken Stock (page 118)
1	tablespoon sesame seeds

Sauce

¼ cup apple juice concentrate

2 teaspoons Ginger Paste (page 117)

1 cup freshly squeezed orange juice

¾ cup dry sherry

1 tablespoon low-salt soy sauce

grated rind of an orange

2 tablespoons cornflour

Preparation

Season wok with canola oil.

Combine parsnip and carrot.

Combine sauce ingredients and mix together well.

Cooking

Add parsnip, carrot and stock to a hot wok and stirfry until vegetables are tender and a vibrant colour.

Add sauce, stir, and cook until sauce thickens.

Transfer to a hot platter and sprinkle with sesame seeds. Serve with rice or noodles. Alternatively, make the dish an accompaniment to barbecued meats or other main courses.

Sesame carrot, zucchini and parsnip in citrus sauce

Serves 4–6

½ cup Chicken Stock (page 118)
350 g carrots, cut into julienne strips
400 g zucchini, topped, tailed and cut into julienne strips
300 g parsnip, peeled and cut into julienne strips
1 tablespoon sesame seeds

Sauce
1 cup freshly squeezed orange juice
1½ cups Chicken Stock (page 118)
1 tablespoon lemon juice
1 tablespoon apple juice concentrate
3 tablespoons cornflour

Preparation
Season wok with canola oil.

Combine prepared vegetables.

Combine sauce ingredients and mix together well.

Cooking
Put chicken stock and vegetables into a hot wok and stirfry for about two minutes or until vegetables are just tender and a vibrant colour.

Add sauce ingredients, stir, and cook for about three minutes.

Transfer to a hot platter and sprinkle with sesame seeds. Serve with rice, couscous or noodles.

Sri Lankan hot vegetable curry

Serves 4–6

1 kg	potatoes, washed and cubed
200 g	carrots, cubed
100 g	parsnip, peeled and cubed
100 g	peas, fresh or frozen
1	onion, peeled and diced
1	teaspoon Garlic Paste (page 117)
1	tablespoon Ginger Paste (page 117)
1	tablespoon ground coriander
1	teaspoon chilli powder
1	teaspoon turmeric
1	teaspoon five-spice powder
1	× 200 ml firm low-fat yoghurt or low-fat sour cream

Sauce

2 tablespoons tomato paste

1 tablespoon cornflour

1½ cups Chicken Stock (page 118)

Preparation

Season wok with canola oil.

Combine onion, garlic paste and ginger paste.

Combine coriander, chilli, turmeric and five-spice powder.

Combine sauce ingredients and mix together well.

Cooking

Steam all vegetables separately until just tender. Run under cold water and leave to become cold.

Add onion, garlic paste and ginger paste to a hot, dry wok and stirfry for about a minute or until onion becomes soft and transparent.

Reduce heat, add spices, and continue cooking for about a minute.

Add potatoes and stirfry for about a minute or until they are well coated with spices. Add sauce, stir, and cook until sauce thickens.

Add remaining vegetables and cook until they are warmed through.

Remove wok from heat and fold yoghurt through the mixture before serving, or serve it separately.

Transfer to a hot platter and serve with rice or a tossed green salad.

Tofu in chilli sauce

Serves 4–6

1 litre water
1 × 2-cm piece fresh ginger, peeled
800 g fresh soft tofu
1 red capsicum, seeded and chopped
1 onion, peeled and sliced
2 spring onions, diagonally sliced

Sauce

1 teaspoon Ginger Paste (page 117)

1 teaspoon Garlic Paste (page 117)

1 tablespoon mirin

3 teaspoons sweet chilli sauce

1½ cups Chicken Stock (page 118)

Preparation

Season wok with canola oil.

Cut tofu into 1-cm cubes.

Combine capsicum and onion.

Combine sauce ingredients.

Cooking

In a large saucepan, bring water and ginger to the boil. Add tofu and simmer gently for about two minutes. Use a slotted spoon to remove tofu; set aside and keep warm.

Boil, steam or microwave capsicum and onion until soft. Drain well. Place in a blender with sauce ingredients and purée until smooth.

Put puréed sauce into a moderately hot wok, stir, and cook for about two minutes or until sauce thickens.

Add spring onions and tofu.

Transfer to a hot platter and serve with a tossed green salad.

*C*hinese vegetable
combination

Serves 4–6

150 g   oyster mushrooms
  2   tablespoons tomato paste
  2   tablespoons low-salt soy sauce
  1   tablespoon Ginger Paste (page 117)
 ¾   cup unsweetened pineapple juice
 ¼   cup dry white wine
 50 g   button mushrooms, halved
200 g   carrot, sliced
100 g   celery, sliced
200 g   red capsicum, seeded and sliced
200 g   sugar peas, topped and tailed
200 g   broccoli, cut into florets
200 g   Chinese cabbage, chopped
400 g   baby corn
  1   × 230 g can water chestnuts, well drained
  1   tablespoon cornflour
 ½   cup water

Preparation
Season wok with canola oil.

Soak oyster mushrooms for twenty minutes. Drain well and slice.

Combine tomato paste, soy sauce, ginger paste, pineapple juice
and wine.

Combine prepared vegetables.

Combine cornflour and water and mix together well.

Cooking
Put tomato paste, soy sauce, ginger, pineapple juice and wine
into a moderately hot wok and cook for about a minute.

Add vegetables and stirfry for about two minutes or until they are just tender and a vibrant colour.

Add water chestnuts.

Add cornflour mixture, stir, and cook until sauce thickens.

Transfer to a hot platter and serve with rice or rice noodles.

Tofu with vegetables

Serves 4–6

500 g	fresh soft tofu
1	litre water
1	× 2-cm piece fresh ginger, peeled
100 g	broccoli, thinly sliced
100 g	cauliflower, thinly sliced
100 g	French beans, halved
200 g	carrots, thinly sliced
100 g	mushrooms, halved
½	cup Chicken Stock (page 118)
1	red capsicum, seeded
½	onion, peeled and sliced
2	spring onions, diagonally sliced

Sauce

1 teaspoon ginger

1 teaspoon garlic

1 tablespoon finely chopped fresh coriander

1 tablespoon mirin

1 tablespoon low-salt soy sauce

1½ cups Chicken Stock (page 118)

1 teaspoon cornflour

Preparation

Season wok with canola oil.

Cut tofu into 1-cm cubes.

Combine capsicum and onion.

Combine sauce ingredients and mix together well.

Cooking

Bring water and ginger to the boil in a large saucepan. Add tofu and simmer gently for about two minutes. Use a slotted spoon to remove tofu; set aside and keep warm.

Add vegetables and chicken stock to a hot wok and stirfry until vegetables are just tender and a vibrant colour.

While vegetables are cooking, boil, steam or microwave capsicum and onion until soft. Drain well. Place in a blender with sauce ingredients and purée until smooth.

Add puréed sauce to wok with vegetables; stir, and cook until sauce thickens.

Add spring onions and tofu.

Transfer to a hot platter and serve with a tossed green salad.

Chow mein of vegetables

Serves 4–6

250 g	thin spaghetti
2	cups Chicken Stock or Vegetable Stock (both page 118) or water
1	onion, peeled and sliced
125 g	celery, diagonally sliced
125 g	sugar peas, topped and tailed
200 g	baby corn
200 g	broccoli florets
100 g	green capsicum, seeded and sliced
100 g	red capsicum, seeded and sliced
100 g	mushrooms, thinly sliced
100 g	bean sprouts

Sauce

2 tablespoons sweet chilli sauce

2 tablespoons low-salt soy sauce

2 tablespoons dry sherry

2 tablespoons cornflour

2 tablespoons water

Preparation

Season wok with canola oil.

Combine prepared vegetables except for bean sprouts.

Combine all sauce ingredients and mix together well.

Cooking

Cook spaghetti until al dente; drain and keep warm.

Put vegetables and stock into a hot wok, cover, and simmer for about a minute or until vegetables are just tender and a vibrant colour.

Reduce heat, add sauce ingredients, stir, and cook until sauce thickens slightly.

Add bean sprouts.

Arrange spaghetti on a hot serving platter and top with the vegetable chow mein.

Vegetable curry

Serves 4–6

1 kg   mixed vegetables, including any of the following: carrot,
       broccoli, zucchini, squash, red capsicum, French beans,
       sugar peas, celery, cauliflower and brussel sprouts – all
       washed and cut into bite-size pieces
2   tablespoons Chicken Stock (page 118)
1   onion, peeled and finely diced
1   teaspoon Garlic Paste (page 117)
1   teaspoon Ginger Paste (page 117)
2   tablespoons finely chopped fresh coriander

Sauce

1 teaspoon turmeric

1 teaspoon coriander

1 teaspoon garam masala

1 teaspoon cumin

1½ cups low-fat milk or soymilk

1 tablespoon cornflour

Preparation

Season wok with canola oil.

Combine prepared vegetables.

Combine chicken stock, onion, garlic paste and ginger paste.

Combine turmeric, coriander, garam masala, cumin, milk and
cornflour, and mix together well.

Cooking

Steam vegetables until just tender and a vibrant colour. Run
under cold water and drain well.

Put stock, onion, garlic paste and ginger paste into a moderately
hot wok and stirfry for about two minutes or until onion is soft
and transparent.

Add sauce ingredients, stir, and cook until sauce thickens.

Return vegetables to wok and cook until they are warmed
through and coated with sauce.

Add coriander.

Transfer to a hot platter and serve with rice, toasted pita bread
or a tossed green salad.

Vegetables in curried carrot sauce

Serves 4–6

500 g sweet potato, peeled and cubed
400 g baby yellow squash, sliced
1 onion, peeled and sliced
½ cup Chicken Stock (page 118) or water
200 g carrot, chopped
½ onion, peeled and sliced
½ yellow capsicum, seeded and sliced
2 teaspoons finely chopped fresh coriander

Sauce

1 teaspoon Ginger Paste (page 117)

1 teaspoon Garlic Paste (page 117)

1 teaspoon Vindaloo curry paste

1 teaspoon cornflour

1 cup Chicken Stock (page 118) or water

Preparation

Season wok with canola oil.

Combine sweet potato, squash and onion.

Combine carrot, onion and capsicum.

Combine sauce ingredients and mix together well.

Cooking

Put sweet potato, squash, onion and chicken stock into a hot wok and stirfry until vegetables are just tender and a vibrant colour.

While these vegetables are cooking in wok, boil, steam or microwave carrot, onion and capsicum together until soft. Drain well. Place in a blender with sauce ingredients and purée until smooth.

Add puréed sauce to wok with vegetables; stir, and cook until sauce thickens. Add coriander.

Transfer to a hot platter and serve with rice, noodles or a tossed green salad.

Vegetable noodles in honey and soy

Serves 4–6

250 g carrot, cut into very thin, long strips
200 g parsnip, peeled and cut into very thin, long strips
250 g zucchini, peeled and cut into very thin, long strips
200 g cucumber, peeled, seeded and cut into very thin, long strips
½ cup Chicken Stock (page 118) or water
3 spring onions, diagonally sliced

Sauce

1 tablespoon Ginger Paste (page 117)

2 tablespoons low-salt soy sauce

1 tablespoon honey

1 tablespoon cornflour

1 cup Chicken Stock (page 118) or water

Preparation

Season wok with canola oil.

Combine prepared vegetables.

Combine sauce ingredients and mix together well.

Cooking

Put vegetables and stock into a hot wok and stirfry until vegetables are just tender and a vibrant colour.

Add sauce, stir, and cook until sauce thickens.

Transfer to a hot platter and garnish with spring onions. Serve with rice and/or a tossed green salad. Alternatively, make the dish an accompaniment to barbecued meats or other main courses.

Spaghetti springs with tomato, pumpkin and olive sauce

Serves 4–6

250 g spaghetti springs (or tomato and basil wheat-free or gluten-free macaroni)
1 Spanish onion, peeled and finely diced
200 g pumpkin, peeled and finely diced
10 black olives, stoned and diced
1 cup dry white wine
500 g fresh tomatoes, seeded, peeled and chopped
¼ teaspoon chilli powder
1 teaspoon dried basil
black pepper
sprigs of fresh basil

Preparation

Season wok with canola oil.

Combine onion, pumpkin and olives.

Combine tomatoes, chilli powder and dried basil.

Cooking

Cook spaghetti springs in boiling water. Drain and keep warm.

Put onion, pumpkin and olives into a moderately hot, dry wok and stirfry for about a minute.

Add wine and tomato mixture; stir, and cook until tomatoes break down and make a sauce.

Add lots of black pepper.

Add spaghetti springs and stirfry until spaghetti is warmed through.

Transfer to a hot platter and garnish with fresh basil. Serve with a tossed green salad.

Wok ratatouille

Serves 4–6

½ cup Chicken Stock or Vegetable Stock (both page 118)
or water
1 teaspoon Garlic Paste (page 117)
2 eggplant, coarsely chopped
1 teaspoon salt
1 onion, peeled and cut into wedges
1 green zucchini, cut into rounds
1 yellow zucchini, cut into rounds
1 green capsicum, seeded and chopped
1 red capsicum, seeded and chopped
10 French beans, halved
1 carrot, cut into rounds
4 tomatoes, peeled and chopped
1 tablespoon each of finely chopped basil and parsley
2 teaspoons finely chopped fresh thyme
black pepper

Preparation

Season wok with canola oil.

Place eggplant and salt in a bowl, cover with water and stand for one hour. Drain and rinse under cold water to remove bitter juices. Drain well.

Combine prepared vegetables.

Combine tomatoes, basil, parsley and thyme.

Cooking

Put stock, garlic paste and eggplant into a hot wok and stirfry for about thirty seconds.

Add all other vegetables. Stirfry for about three minutes or until vegetables begin to soften and are a vibrant colour.

Reduce heat, then add tomatoes and herbs and stirfry for two minutes. Cover and cook gently until vegetables are very tender and sauce thickens.

Lift lid and stir occasionally so that vegetables do not stick to base of wok. Season with black pepper to taste.

Transfer to a hot platter and serve with rice, pasta or crusty bread. Alternatively, make the dish an accompaniment to your main course.

Vegetarian tofu sukiyaki

Serves 4–6

3 cups Vegetable Stock (page 118) or water
1 teaspoon grated lemon rind
400 g firm tofu
200 g carrots, thinly sliced
100 g broccoli, thinly sliced
100 g French beans, diagonally sliced
200 g bok choy, roughly chopped
100 g mushrooms, thinly sliced
2 spring onions, thinly sliced diagonally

Sauce
¼ cup mirin

⅓ cup Vegetable Stock (page 118) or water

1 tablespoon apple juice concentrate

½ teaspoon Garlic Paste (page 117)

Preparation

Season wok with canola oil.

Cut tofu into 2-cm cubes.

Combine all prepared vegetables except spring onions.

Cooking

Pour stock into wok and heat until just simmering.

Add tofu and simmer gently for a minute or until it is heated through. Use a slotted spoon to remove tofu from wok; keep it warm.

Wipe out wok, add sauce ingredients, stir, and cook over moderate heat for about two minutes or until sauce reduces by half.

Add vegetables, cover, and cook for about two minutes or until they are just tender and a vibrant colour.

Return warm tofu to wok and gently combine with the other ingredients, being careful not to break up the tofu.

Transfer to a hot platter and garnish with spring onions. Serve with pasta.

Peaches and apricots in passionfruit sauce

Serves 4–6

¼ cup slivered almonds
4 fresh peaches, peeled, stoned and halved
8 fresh apricots, stoned and halved
  pulp of 6 passionfruit
1 tablespoon cornflour
½ cup water

Sauce
1 cup freshly squeezed or unsweetened orange juice

1 tablespoon sugar-free marmalade

Preparation

Season wok with canola oil.

Combine sauce ingredients.

Combine prepared fruit.

Combine cornflour and water and mix together well.

Cooking

Put almonds into a moderately hot, dry wok and stirfry for a few seconds until they are golden brown. Remove from wok.

Add sauce ingredients to wok and stir for about two minutes.

Add peaches and apricots and cook for about a minute.

Stir in passionfruit pulp.

Add cornflour mixture, stir, and cook until sauce thickens.

Top with slivered almonds.

Serve hot or cold with low-fat icecream. Alternatively, spoon over pancakes or porridge.

Mango and banana
with creamy coconut sauce

Serves 4–6

2 mangoes, peeled and sliced
3 bananas, peeled and diagonally sliced
1 tablespoon cornflour
½ cup light coconut milk

Sauce

1 cup freshly
squeezed or
unsweetened
orange juice

grated rind of an
orange

2 tablespoons
Galliano liqueur

Preparation

Season wok with canola oil.

Combine sauce ingredients.

Combine prepared fruit.

Combine cornflour and coconut milk and mix together well.

Cooking

Put sauce ingredients into a moderately hot wok and stir for about two minutes or until sauce is slightly reduced.

Add fruit and cook gently to just warm through. Add cornflour mixture, stir and cook until sauce thickens.

Serve hot or cold with low-fat icecream or over pancakes.

Banana, lychees and mango

Serves 4–6

3   bananas, peeled and diagonally sliced
1   × 565 g can lychees in light syrup, well drained
1   mango, peeled and segmented
1   tablespoon cornflour
¼   cup reserved lychee syrup or water

Sauce

¾ cup freshly squeezed or unsweetened orange juice

2 tablespoons sugar-free marmalade

Preparation

Season wok with canola oil.

Combine sauce ingredients.

Combine cornflour and lychee syrup and mix together well.

Cooking

Put sauce ingredients into a moderately hot wok and stir for about two minutes or until sauce is slightly reduced.

Add bananas, lychees and mango and cook for about a minute.

Add cornflour mixture, stir, and cook until sauce thickens.

Serve hot or cold with low-fat icecream, over pancakes or with porridge.

Hot tropical
ginger fruit salad

Serves 6

½ cantaloupe, peeled and sliced
½ honeydew melon, peeled and sliced
1 mango, peeled and sliced
400 g fresh pineapple, peeled and sliced
1 cup green grapes
1 cup black grapes
1 cup cherries, stones removed
1 tablespoon cornflour
½ cup water

Sauce

½ cup green ginger wine

½ cup water

grated rind of an orange

grated rind of a lime

1 cinnamon stick

Preparation

Season wok with canola oil.

Combine sauce ingredients.

Combine prepared fruit.

Combine cornflour and water and mix together well.

Cooking

Put sauce ingredients into a moderately hot wok and stir for about two minutes or until slightly reduced. Remove cinnamon stick.

Add fruit and cook gently to just warm through.

Add cornflour mixture, stir and cook until sauce thickens.

Serve hot or cold with low-fat icecream.

Fruits with creamy ginger coconut sauce

Serves 4–6

2	bananas, peeled and diagonally sliced
500 g	fresh pineapple, peeled and sliced
6	fresh nectarines, stoned and halved
1	tablespoon cornflour
½	cup light coconut milk
1	tablespoon toasted shredded coconut

Sauce

1 cup freshly squeezed or unsweetened orange juice

2 tablespoons diced glacé ginger

1 tablespoon green ginger wine

Preparation

Season wok with canola oil.

Combine sauce ingredients.

Combine prepared fruit.

Combine cornflour and coconut milk and mix together well.

Cooking

Put sauce ingredients into a moderately hot wok and stir for about two minutes or until sauce is slightly reduced.

Add fruit and cook gently to just warm through.

Add cornflour mixture and stir until thickened.

Top with coconut.

Serve hot or cold with low-fat icecream or over pancakes.

Winter warmers

Nourishing noodle dishes, risottos
and even soups can be made
in the wok to help sustain you
on cool days. All are low
in fat but rich in carbohydrates,
fibre and flavour.

Noodles with chilli beef
and capsicum

Serves 4–6

250 g	noodles
400 g	beef fillet, trimmed of fat and cut into thin strips
1	teaspoon Garlic Paste (page 117)
1	onion, peeled and sliced
2	tablespoons low-salt soy sauce
1	tablespoon hoi sin sauce
2	small red chillies, seeded and chopped
1	cup Beef Stock or Chicken Stock (both page 118)
1	tablespoon apple juice concentrate
100 g	yellow capsicum, seeded and cut into strips
100 g	green capsicum, seeded and cut into strips
200 g	red capsicum, seeded and cut into strips
1	teaspoon cornflour
1	tablespoon water
	sprigs of fresh coriander

Preparation

Season wok with canola oil and garlic clove.

Combine beef, garlic paste, onion, soy sauce, hoi sin sauce and chillies and mix together well. Allow to stand for at least an hour.

Combine stock and apple juice concentrate.

Combine strips of capsicum.

Combine cornflour and water and mix together well.

Cooking

Cook noodles in boiling water until al dente. Drain and run cold water through them. Drain well.

Put beef mixture into a hot, dry wok and stirfry for about two minutes or until beef loses its raw exterior colour and onion becomes transparent. Remove beef mixture from wok and set aside to keep warm.

Reduce heat, add stock, apple juice concentrate and capsicum, and stirfry for about two minutes or until capsicum is just tender and a vibrant colour.

Add cornflour mixture, stir and cook until sauce begins to thicken. Add noodles and toss them through the sauce. Add beef and stirfry all ingredients until they are evenly mixed and noodles and beef are warmed through.

Transfer to a hot platter and garnish with fresh coriander. Serve with a tossed green salad.

Noodles with hot
spicy pumpkin and peas

Serves 4–6

600 g   pumpkin, peeled and cubed
1   tablespoon Ginger Paste (page 117)
2   teaspoons Vindaloo curry paste
¼   cup tomato paste
300 g   noodles
½   cup Vegetable Stock or Chicken Stock (both page 118)
½   cup freshly squeezed orange juice
1   extra teaspoon Ginger Paste (page 117)
1   teaspoon finely chopped fresh lemon grass
2   teaspoons cornflour
1   cup cooked peas
2   tablespoons dry-roasted pine nuts
  sprigs of fresh coriander

Preparation

Season wok with canola oil.

Combine ginger paste, curry paste and tomato paste.

Combine stock, orange juice, extra ginger paste, lemon grass and cornflour and mix together well.

Cooking

Cook pumpkin until soft; drain and leave to go cold.

Place cold pumpkin in a bowl with ginger paste, curry paste and tomato paste and coat well.

Spoon pumpkin onto a non-stick baking tray and bake in a hot oven for a few minutes, or put under a griller until it crisps up. Set aside and keep warm.

Cook noodles in boiling water until al dente. Drain and run cold water through them. Drain well.

Reduce heat and add stock, orange juice, ginger paste, lemon grass and cornflour. Stir and cook for about two minutes or until sauce begins to thicken.

Add noodles, peas and pumpkin and toss until all ingredients are warmed through.

Transfer to a hot platter and garnish with pine nuts and fresh coriander. Serve with a tossed green salad.

Noodles Thai-style with water chestnuts

Serves 4–6

300 g   noodles
½   onion, peeled and finely diced
1   teaspoon Garlic Paste (page 117)
2   tablespoons low-salt soy sauce
2   small red chillies, seeded and finely chopped
2   tablespoons wine vinegar
2   tablespoons lime juice
1   × 230 g can water chestnuts, drained and sliced
200 g   bean sprouts
2   tablespoons finely chopped fresh coriander
    extra bean sprouts

Preparation

Season wok with canola oil.

Combine onion, garlic paste, soy sauce, chillies, vinegar and lime juice.

Cooking

Cook noodles in boiling water until al dente. Drain and run cold water through them. Drain well.

Put onion, garlic paste, soy sauce, chillies, vinegar and lime juice into a moderately hot wok and stirfry for about two minutes or until onion becomes transparent.

Reduce heat, add water chestnuts and toss lightly.

Add bean sprouts, noodles and coriander and stirfry until all ingredients are warmed through.

Transfer to a hot platter and garnish with extra bean sprouts. Serve with a tossed green salad.

Mussels in basilica tomato sauce with noodles

Serves 4–6

1	quantity Basilica Tomato Sauce (page 116)
250 g	noodles
1	litre water
2 kg	mussels
1	onion, peeled and sliced
1	teaspoon Garlic Paste (page 117)
2	small red chillies, seeded and finely chopped
1	teaspoon sweet chilli sauce
2	green capsicums, seeded and chopped
2	tablespoons dry white wine
4	spring onions, diagonally sliced
2	tablespoons finely chopped fresh parsley
	black pepper
	sprigs of fresh basil

Preparation

Season wok with canola oil.

Prepare mussels by pulling away the beard and use a stiff brush to scrub them under cold running water to remove grit.

Combine onion, garlic paste, chillies, chilli sauce and capsicum.

Cooking

In a small saucepan heat tomato sauce to simmering point and keep warm.

Cook noodles in boiling water until al dente. Drain and run cold water through them. Drain well.

Put the litre of water into a hot wok and bring to the boil. Position a steaming rack over the water and add mussels. Cover, and steam mussels to open them. As they open, remove and set aside to keep warm. Keep intact three mussels per person and

→

remove remaining mussels from their shells. Discard any that do not open after five minutes.

Wipe out wok and season again with canola oil.

Add onion, garlic paste, chillies, chilli sauce and capsicum to hot, dry wok. Stirfry for about a minute or until onion becomes transparent and capsicum just tender and a vibrant colour. Add wine.

Add tomato sauce, stir and cook until sauce begins to bubble. Add noodles and toss until they are warmed through.

Add spring onions, parsley and black pepper to taste.

Transfer to a hot platter and garnish with fresh basil. Serve with a tossed green salad.

Sweet bok choy
with noodles

Serves 4–6

300 g	noodles
½	onion, peeled and finely diced
1	tablespoon Ginger Paste (page 117)
2	tablespoons low-salt soy sauce
2	tablespoons dry sherry
2	small red chillies, seeded and finely chopped
1	cup Vegetable Stock or Chicken Stock (both page 118)
1	tablespoon apple juice concentrate
500 g	bok choy, washed and chopped
100 g	carrot, peeled and cut into thin rounds
2	teaspoons cornflour
2	tablespoons water
100 g	bean sprouts
1	tablespoon finely chopped fresh coriander
	sprigs of fresh coriander

Preparation

Season wok with canola oil.

Combine onion, ginger paste, soy sauce, sherry and chillies.

Combine prepared bok choy and carrot.

Combine stock and apple juice concentrate.

Combine cornflour and water and mix together well.

Combine bean sprouts and coriander.

Cooking

Cook noodles in boiling water until al dente. Drain and run cold water through them. Drain well.

➥

Put onion, ginger paste, soy sauce, sherry and chillies into a hot, dry wok and stirfry for about a minute or until onion is soft and transparent.

Stir in stock and apple juice concentrate.

Add bok choy and carrot and stirfry for about two minutes or until they are just tender and a vibrant colour. Add cornflour mixture, stir and cook until sauce begins to thicken.

Add noodles, bean sprouts and chopped coriander and toss until all ingredients are warmed through.

Transfer to a hot platter and garnish with sprigs of coriander. Serve with a tossed green salad.

Noodles with tuscan tomato sauce and vegetables

Serves 4–6

1   quantity Tuscan Tomato Sauce (page 117)
250 g   noodles
200 g   snow peas, topped and tailed
1   cup water
400 g   mushrooms, thinly sliced
2   tablespoons dry white wine
100 g   sundried tomatoes, well drained
8   spring onions, diagonally sliced
    black pepper
    sprigs of fresh basil

Preparation

Season wok with canola oil.

Prepare all ingredients as listed.

Cooking

In a small saucepan heat tomato sauce to simmering point and keep warm.

Cook noodles in boiling water until al dente. Drain and run cold water through them. Drain well.

Put cup of water into a hot wok and bring to the boil. Add snow peas and simmer for about a minute or until they are just tender and a vibrant green. Use a slotted spoon to remove snow peas and run under cold water. Set aside.

Wipe out wok and season again with canola oil.

Put mushrooms and wine into hot, dry wok and stirfry for about a minute or until mushrooms are soft.

Reduce heat and stir in sundried tomatoes and spring onions, quickly followed by sauce. Stir and cook until sauce begins to bubble.

Add noodles and snow peas and toss until noodles are warmed through. Add black pepper to taste.

Transfer to a hot platter and garnish with fresh basil. Serve with a tossed green salad.

Capsicum and crab risotto

Serves 4

200 g   red capsicum, seeded and diced
100 g   zucchini, diced
4   cups cooked brown rice
2   extra cups Chicken Stock (page 118)
300 g   crab meat
2   tablespoons grated parmesan cheese
1   tablespoon finely chopped fresh dill
black pepper
sprigs of fresh dill

Cooking stock
1 cup Chicken Stock (page 118)

1 teaspoon Ginger Paste (page 117)

1 teaspoon dried dill

Preparation

Season wok with canola oil.

Combine prepared vegetables.

Combine cooking stock ingredients.

Cooking

Put vegetables and cooking stock into a moderately hot wok and gently stirfry for about three minutes or until capsicum and zucchini begin to soften.

Add one cup of rice and about half a cup of extra chicken stock, and stir until stock has evaporated.

Add another cup of rice and the same amount of chicken stock, and again stir until all stock has evaporated.

Repeat this process until all rice and chicken stock has been added to the risotto. Add crab meat with the last lot of rice and stock, and stir it through the rice until all stock has evaporated (the warm rice will cook the crab).

Remove risotto from heat and stir in parmesan cheese and chopped dill, then season with black pepper to taste. Serve on individual platters garnished with sprigs of dill.

Chicken and asparagus risotto

Serves 4

400 g   chicken fillet, skin and fat removed
1   onion, peeled and diced
200 g   asparagus spears, diagonally sliced
3   cups cooked brown rice
1½   extra cups Chicken Stock (page 118)
¼   cup chopped sundried tomatoes, well drained
2   tablespoons grated parmesan cheese
¼   cup chopped spring onions
1   teaspoon finely chopped fresh coriander
  sprigs of fresh coriander

Cooking stock
1 cup Chicken Stock (page 118)

½ cup dry white wine

1 teaspoon Ginger Paste (page 117)

Preparation

Season wok with canola oil.

Dice chicken into very small pieces.

Combine prepared vegetables.

Combine cooking stock ingredients.

Cooking

Put chicken and cooking stock into a moderately hot wok; cover, and simmer for about two minutes or until chicken is lightly poached.

Remove chicken from wok and set aside to keep warm.

Add vegetables and stirfry for about two minutes or until they are soft.

Add one cup of rice and about half a cup of extra chicken stock, and stir until stock has evaporated.

Add another cup of rice and the same amount of chicken stock, and again stir until all stock has evaporated. Repeat this process until all rice and chicken stock has been added to the risotto.

Return cooked chicken to wok with the last lot of rice and stock. Stir it through the rice until all stock has evaporated.

Remove risotto from heat and stir in sundried tomatoes, parmesan cheese, spring onions and chopped coriander.

Serve on individual platters garnished with sprigs of coriander.

Mushroom and broccoli risotto

Serves 4

300 g mushrooms, washed and thinly sliced
4 cups cooked brown rice
2 cups Chicken Stock (page 118)
200 g broccoli, cut into florets
2 tablespoons grated parmesan cheese
2 tablespoons finely chopped chives
black pepper
sprigs of fresh coriander

Cooking stock
1 cup dry white wine

1 tablespoon chopped fresh basil leaves

1 tablespoon chopped fresh dill

Preparation
Season wok with canola oil.

Combine cooking stock ingredients.

Cooking
Put mushrooms and cooking stock into a moderately hot wok and gently stirfry for about three minutes or until mushrooms begin to soften.

Add one cup of rice and about half a cup of chicken stock, and stir until stock has evaporated.

Add another cup of rice and the same amount of chicken stock, and again stir until all stock has evaporated.

Repeat this process until all rice and chicken stock has been added to the risotto.

Add broccoli with the last lot of rice and stock.

Stir until all stock has evaporated and broccoli is tender and a vibrant green.

Remove risotto from heat and stir in parmesan cheese and chives, then season with black pepper to taste. Serve on individual platters garnished with coriander.

Pumpkin
and pea risotto

Serves 4

300 g pumpkin, peeled and diced
1 cup fresh or frozen peas
4 cups cooked brown rice
2 cups Chicken Stock (page 118)
2 tablespoons grated parmesan cheese
   black pepper
   sprigs of fresh coriander

Cooking stock
1 cup freshly squeezed or unsweetened orange juice

1 teaspoon sweet chilli sauce

a few sprigs of fresh coriander

Preparation

Season wok with canola oil.

Combine prepared vegetables.

Combine cooking stock ingredients.

Cooking

Put vegetables and cooking stock into a moderately hot wok and gently stirfry for about three minutes or until pumpkin and peas begin to soften.

Add one cup of rice and about half a cup of chicken stock and stir until stock has evaporated.

Add another cup of rice and the same amount of chicken stock, and again stir until all stock has evaporated.

Repeat this process until all rice and chicken stock has been added to the risotto. Stir until all stock has evaporated.

Remove risotto from heat and stir in parmesan cheese, then season with black pepper to taste. Serve on individual platters garnished with the extra coriander.

Sweet potato and artichoke risotto

Serves 4

400 g sweet potato, peeled and diced
4 cups cooked brown rice
2 cups Chicken Stock (page 118)
1 × 400 g can artichoke hearts, well drained and cut in half
2 tablespoons grated parmesan cheese
1 tablespoon finely chopped fresh coriander
2 tablespoons finely chopped chives
   sprigs of fresh coriander

Cooking stock
1 cup freshly squeezed or unsweetened orange juice

1 teaspoon Ginger Paste (page 117)

½ teaspoon Garlic Paste (page 117)

1 teaspoon Vindaloo curry paste

Preparation

Season wok with canola oil.

Combine cooking stock ingredients.

Cooking

Put sweet potato and cooking stock into a moderately hot wok and gently stirfry for about three minutes or until sweet potato begins to soften.

Add one cup of rice and about half a cup of chicken stock, and stir until stock has evaporated.

Add another cup of rice and the same amount of chicken stock, and again stir until all stock has evaporated.

Repeat this process until all rice and chicken stock has been added to the risotto. Stir until all stock has evaporated.

At the very last moment, add artichoke hearts to wok and stir into the risotto to warm through.

Remove risotto from heat and stir in parmesan cheese, chives and chopped coriander. Serve on individual platters garnished with sprigs of coriander.

Chicken and vegetable soup

Serves 6

300 g	diced chicken, skin and fat removed
1	teaspoon Ginger Paste (page 117)
1	teaspoon Garlic Paste (page 117)
1	teaspoon grated lemon rind
1	onion, peeled and sliced
2	cups Chicken Stock (page 118)
100 g	celery, sliced
100 g	carrots, cut into rounds
100 g	red capsicum, seeded and chopped
100 g	French beans, topped, tailed and halved
100 g	corn kernels
1	quantity Tuscan Tomato Sauce (page 117)
½	cup dry white wine
1	teaspoon finely chopped fresh coriander
1	teaspoon finely chopped fresh lemon grass

Preparation

Season wok with canola oil.

Combine chicken, ginger paste, garlic paste, lemon rind and onion.

Combine prepared vegetables.

Cooking

Put chicken mixture into a hot, dry wok and stirfry for about three minutes or until chicken loses its raw exterior colour and onion becomes transparent.

Remove chicken from wok and set aside to keep warm.

Add stock to wok and bring to the boil.

Add vegetables and simmer until they are just tender and a vibrant colour. Stir occasionally so that vegetables do not stick to base of wok.

Add sauce and wine and stir until soup begins to simmer.

Add cooked chicken and herbs, and continue to cook for a few minutes or until chicken is warmed through.

Serve with hot, crusty brown bread.

Rip fish soup

Serves 6

1	quantity Marinara Tomato Sauce (page 116)
100 g	carrot, peeled and cut into thin strips
100 g	zucchini, cut into thin strips
1	cup dry white wine
500 g	prawns
100 g	scallops
200 g	thick white fish fillets, cut into bite-size pieces
2	tablespoons finely chopped fresh mixed herbs (parsley, basil, coriander and chives)
	black pepper

Cooking stock

1 cup dry white wine

4 cups water

1 onion, peeled and sliced

2 carrots, peeled and chopped

1 stick celery, chopped

a few sprigs fresh coriander or parsley

Preparation

Season wok with canola oil.

Peel prawns (keep shells for stock) and remove sac from scallops. Combine prawns, scallops and fish pieces.

Combine cooking stock ingredients.

Combine prepared vegetables.

Cooking

Put cooking stock and prawn shells into a moderately hot wok; cover and simmer for fifteen minutes.

Strain stock and reserve two cups. (For a richer-flavoured soup you can return strained stock to a hot wok and simmer to reduce to two cups.)

Heat marinara sauce to simmering point in a small saucepan and keep hot.

Season wok with canola oil.

Put vegetables into hot, dry wok and stirfry for about thirty seconds or until they become soft. Add a little stock or water if vegetables stick to base of wok.

Add wine and stirfry for another thirty seconds.

Add reserved cooking stock and bring to a gentle simmer.

Add combined fish and gently simmer for about three minutes or until fish is just tender.

Stir in marinara sauce and fresh herbs, and add black pepper to taste. Serve with hot, crusty brown bread.

Surfers vegetable soup

Serves 6

1   quantity Tuscan Tomato Sauce (page 117)
1   onion, peeled and sliced
200 g   potatoes, peeled and cubed
200 g   pumpkin, peeled and cubed
100 g   sweet potato, peeled and cubed
100 g   zucchini, cut into rounds
100 g   carrots, peeled and cut into thin strips
100 g   French beans, topped, tailed and halved
100 g   celery, sliced
2   tablespoons finely chopped fresh mixed herbs (parsley, thyme, marjoram and chives)
    black pepper

Cooking stock

1 litre Vegetable, Beef or Chicken Stock (page 118)

1 teaspoon Garlic Paste (page 117)

a few sprigs fresh coriander or parsley

Preparation

Season wok with canola oil.

Combine cooking stock ingredients.

Combine onion, potato, pumpkin and sweet potato.

Combine zucchini, carrots, beans and celery.

Cooking

Heat tomato sauce to simmering point in a small saucepan and keep warm.

Pour cooking stock into wok and bring to the boil. Add onion, potato, pumpkin and sweet potato and gently simmer, covered, for five minutes. Lift lid and stir occasionally so that vegetables do not stick to base of wok.

Add zucchini, carrots, beans and celery and continue cooking for three minutes or until these vegetables are just tender and a vibrant colour. Remove coriander or parsley.

Add sauce and stir until soup begins to simmer.

Add mixed herbs and black pepper to taste.

Serve with hot, crusty brown bread.

About the ingredients

APPLE JUICE CONCENTRATE   Used as a substitute sweetener, it has a sugar content of about 66 per cent (honey has about 80 per cent). Apple juice concentrate can be substituted for honey in any recipe.

BEEF   Use prime eye-fillet beef, with all visible fat removed.

BLACK PEPPER   Use freshly ground black peppercorns.

CANOLA OIL   Canola oil is used to season the wok before cooking because it tolerates higher temperatures than most other oils.

CHICKEN   Breast fillets, with skin and fat removed, are recommended.

CHILLIES   Red or green chillies may be used; the seeds add extra heat.

COCONUT   Use shredded coconut. To toast, stir the coconut in a small pan over low heat until it begins to change colour.

COCONUT MILK   Canned coconut milk is thinner in consistency than coconut cream and lower in fat. Look for 'light' or 'low-fat' coconut milk or replace half the coconut milk with low-fat milk or water.

CORIANDER PASTE   This is a commercial blend of fresh coriander, vegetable oil, salt and acetic acid.

CURRY PASTE   Of the prepared curry pastes available, I particularly like the Vindaloo brand.

DRIED MUSHROOMS   Dried mushrooms may be substituted for cultivated mushrooms in these recipes. They have a richer flavour and you may need to acquire a taste for them. Soak dried mushrooms for about twenty minutes in hot water, drain well and chop before cooking lightly.

EVAPORATED SKIM MILK   Canned skim milk contains no sugar, has a heavier texture than non-fat milk, and is a good substitute for whole milk. Its fat content is less than 0.5 per cent. The 'light' variety is particularly recommended. Soymilk is a dairy-free alternative.

FIVE-SPICE POWDER   This is a pungent, commercially available combination of cinnamon, cloves, fennel, star anise and Sichuan peppers.

GREEN GINGER WINE   This is a sweet wine infused with ginger.

HERBS   When substituting dry herbs for fresh, observe the following rule: one tablespoon of fresh herbs equals one teaspoon of dried herbs.

HOI SIN SAUCE   This thick Chinese sauce is made from salted black beans, onions and garlic. If you are on a low-sodium diet use it sparingly or replace half the quantity of sauce with water.

LEMON GRASS   Fresh lemon grass has been used in these recipes. Bruise the stem (if using whole) before cooking. Store fresh lemon grass in water, replaced daily. The fresher the lemon grass, the more potent the flavour. You can substitute grated lemon rind for lemon grass, but the flavour will be slightly different.

MIRIN   This is a sweet rice-wine vinegar. A good substitute for mirin is a mixture of 1 part apple juice concentrate, 2 parts water and 1 part dry sherry.

NOODLES   Rice noodles, wheat noodles, or noodles that are free of wheat or gluten are all suitable.

PORK   Use pork fillet with all visible fat removed.

PRAWNS   Use uncooked green prawns.

RICE, WHITE   Served as a main meal accompaniment, it is devoid of fibre and usually balances a meal containing high-fibre vegetables, with or without meat. There are a variety of rices available, all offering different flavours. For a diet higher in fibre, use brown rice to accompany meals.

RICE, BROWN   This is the natural, unpolished rice with bran intact. The bran offers additional protein, plus traces of iron, calcium and Vitamin B. It has a nutty flavour, is extremely nutritious, and takes a little longer to cook than white rice.

SOY SAUCE   A low-salt soy sauce has been used in these recipes. If you are on a low-sodium diet, use it sparingly or replace half the quantity of sauce with water.

TANDOORI PASTE   This is a commercial blend of garlic, tamarind, ginger, coriander, cumin, turmeric, chilli, salt, acetic acid, mixed spices and red colour.

TERIYAKI SAUCE This is a commercial blend of soy sauce, wine, vinegar and spices. If you are on a low-sodium diet, use it sparingly or replace half the quantity of sauce with water.

TOFU Often referred to as bean curd, this is available fresh at supermarkets or delicatessens, and in packets. To make tofu, soymilk is coagulated and the resulting curds are compressed into blocks. It is an excellent protein substitute for meat, being low in fat and cholesterol-free.

TOMATO PASTE Look for low-salt or salt-free varieties.

WATER CHESTNUTS Drain the can and rinse the water chestnuts well to remove salt.

Basic recipes

Tomato sauces

Use the following method for all four tomato sauces. Combine ingredients in a blender and process until smooth. Cook in a small saucepan for about ten minutes or until mixture boils, reduces a little and thickens. This sauce can be prepared ahead of time and stored in the refrigerator, where it will keep for about a week. It can also be frozen.

Basilica Tomato Sauce ingredients

1 onion, peeled and sliced
1 teaspoon Garlic Paste (page 117)
1 × 425 g can tomatoes
$\frac{1}{2}$ cup tomato paste
$\frac{1}{2}$ teaspoon dried basil
$\frac{1}{2}$ teaspoon ground oregano
1 cup dry white wine

Marinara Tomato Sauce ingredients

1 onion, peeled and sliced
1 × 425 g can tomatoes
$\frac{1}{2}$ cup tomato paste
$\frac{1}{2}$ teaspoon dried basil
1 teaspoon dried mint
1 tablespoon finely chopped fresh parsley
1 cup dry white wine

Neapolitan Tomato Sauce ingredients

1 onion, peeled and sliced
1 × 425 g can tomatoes
$\frac{1}{2}$ cup tomato paste
1 teaspoon dried basil
1 teaspoon Chilli, Ginger and Garlic Paste (page 117)
$\frac{1}{2}$ cup dry red wine
$\frac{1}{2}$ cup water

Tuscan Tomato Sauce ingredients
1 onion, peeled and sliced
1 × 425 g can tomatoes
½ cup tomato paste
2 tablespoons finely chopped black olives
1 teaspoon capers
1 teaspoon Garlic Paste (page 117)
1 tablespoon finely chopped fresh parsley
1 cup dry white wine

Pastes
Chilli, Ginger and Garlic Paste
100 g red chillies, green tops removed
20 g fresh ginger, peeled
20 g garlic cloves, peeled

Combine all ingredients in a food processor and blend to a paste. Store in
a sealed container in the refrigerator. This paste will normally last up to
three weeks, but can be preserved longer by adding half a cup of wine
vinegar or good quality virgin oil.

Garlic Paste
Remove the skin from fresh garlic and blend to a paste in a food processor.
Store in a sealed container in the refrigerator. Commercial garlic paste is
also available. Avoid the varieties with added sugar.

Ginger Paste
Remove the skin from fresh ginger and blend to a paste in a food
processor. Store in a sealed container in the refrigerator. Commercial
ginger paste is also available. Avoid the varieties with added sugar.

Stocks
Use the following method for all four stocks. Combine all the ingredients,
place in a large pan, bring to the boil and simmer for about thirty minutes.
Strain stock. For a more intense flavour return stock to a clean pan, bring
to the boil and reduce by half. Use stock as required to add extra flavour
to recipes. Keep stock in a sealed container in the refrigerator or freeze it.

Beef Stock ingredients
1 kg beef bones
1 onion, peeled and sliced
200 g celery, chopped
200 g carrot, chopped
1.5 litres water
6 black peppercorns
1 tablespoon low-salt soy sauce (optional)

Chicken Stock ingredients
1 kg chicken meat, bones or carcasses
1 onion, peeled and chopped
100 g celery, chopped
100 g carrot, chopped
½ cup chopped parsley
1 bay leaf
6 peppercorns
2 teaspoons Ginger Paste (page 117)
1.5 litres water

Fish Stock ingredients
1 kg clean fish-heads, shells, scraps
1.5 litres water
1 cup white wine
2 onions, peeled and sliced
200 g carrot, chopped
½ cup chopped parsley
2 bay leaves

Vegetable Stock ingredients
1 kg chopped mixed vegetables (carrot, celery, onion, pumpkin, potato, parsnip)
1.5 litres water
1 tablespoon tomato paste (optional)
½ cup chopped parsley
2 bay leaves
6 peppercorns

Index